OUT *of the* LABYRINTH

BY
L. H. LEHMANN

Ah, must—Designer Infinite—
Must thou char the wood, ere thou canst limn with it?
—FRANCIS THOMPSON.

✝

Published by Chick Publications
P.O. Box 662, Chino, CA 91710
Printed in the United States of America

1982

Library of Congress Catalog Card No. 82-74116

ISBN: 0-937958-13-1

TO THE LORD AND SAVIOUR

this work is thankfully dedicated

With acknowledgment to

F.M.

Whose spiritual insight helped with

many parts of it

PUBLISHER'S FOREWORD

Of the few priests who escape the Roman system, L. H. Lehmann is one of the most knowledgeable about its intricate deceptions. Although his book, **OUT OF THE LABYRINTH,** was written some years ago it provides broad coverage of the basic evils of the system. Since the Vatican claims it never changes, the message of this book is as relevant as ever. Out of print for a number of years, we felt God would have us republish this important work so that modern "protestants" may know more clearly what they must "protest."

TABLE OF CONTENTS

CHAPTER ONE

INTO THE LIGHT

"Our soul is escaped like a bird out of the net of the fowlers: the net is broken and we are escaped"
(Ps. 124).

THE CONVERSION OF A PRIEST is a special kind of conversion — something more than a 'turning around' as the word conversion signifies. It is rather a complete turn-over, a spiritual 'somersault.' It involves a descent from his false position as an *alter Christus*, "another Christ," as he was formerly called, to a humble admission that he is but another sinner saved by Christ.

As a priest, I was hailed as a "mediator between God and man," offering sacrifices daily for the sins of men and forgiving them their sins in confession. I was regarded as indispensable to sinners, since without the priest in Roman Catholic teaching there is no salvation. The change that took place within me by my conversion required a complete repudiation of all this. From my sacerdotal eminence I had to come tumbling down upon my knees to confess that, like all other men, I myself was a sinner needing to be saved by Christ.

Such a conversion is not as simple as it may seem. In the first place, it is entirely against the nature of man so to humble himself as to voluntarily renounce the privileges and power by which he is endowed in such a lofty estate. Nor is such a conversion attained merely by the act of just leaving the Roman priesthood. Neither is it arrived at by intellectual disquisition, the logic of reasoning or the metaphysics of argumentation. If it is hardly possible for a camel to pass through the eye of a needle, it is not at all possible to enter head first into the Kingdom of Heaven.

Apprehension of the truth of Christ with acceptance of Him as personal Saviour is by a sense other than pure intellect; different too from mere emotional affectation. My experience has taught me that it can only come by a spiritual sense, itself a gift of God first implanted in the soul as necessary for the reception of his supreme gift of eternal life—an "act of God" which, like a bolt of lightning, everlastingly fuses the innermost being of a man with his Creator and Saviour. There is nothing in human reasoning, or logic, or history that can otherwise explain it.

How foolish appear now to me those little words, compounded of Greek and Latin to give them a sense of pretended importance, which I learned as a student and a priest and which were supposed to explain and dogmatically prove the mystery of Christian soteriology! As well try to measure the infinite with a twelve-inch ruler.

In my book, *The Soul of a Priest,* I set down objectively the odyssey of my soul during the years of my life as a boy, a student and a priest. Therein were detailed the historical events that finally led to my break with the priesthood of the Church of Rome after serving it well and faithfully on three continents. It is to fill up that history of a soul's further triumphant search for Christian truth that I publish this second book which contains the results of that soul's spiritual development. These writings have been fashioned by my experiences as editor of *The Converted Catholic Magazine* and director of Christ's Mission in New York during the past ten years.

I cannot imagine any more objective or experimental way of showing how completely I have rejected the erroneous teachings and false pretensions of all that I was taught to believe and to teach as a priest. This is all the more clearly demonstrated by the method I use of contrasting the truth with the lie, the genuine with the counterfeit, in all that concerns salvation in the Christian dispensation.

The method followed in these chapters is both legitimate and justifiable. For I soon learned that the Word of God is truly like a two-edged sword definitely cleaving apart the true from the false, the things of God from those of Satan. There are no nuances of Gospel truth as there are of colors. There are no mere half-truths concerning creation and salvation, no half-measures to God's actions. Christianity, I have discovered, is an *either/or* religion. By it you are either saved or not saved, made alive or dead. To say or teach, as I used to in Roman Catholicism, that it is a religion that leaves you at death not good enough for heaven yet not bad enough for hell, is a mockery of logic as well as a mockery of Calvary. It is like squaring the circle to say that at the same time you can be saved and not saved.

It is Satan who has thus made a labyrinth of the Christian religion, with himself as the false guide through the inextricable maze. On men's nose he thrusts the spectacles of falsehood, through which they see everything entirely opposite to what God has ordained and accomplished for our salvation. Distant things appear near, near things distant, small things large, and large things small, ugly things beautiful and beautiful things ugly, white black and black white, life as death and death as life—in short, the mystery of the Cross as foolishness and his own mystery of iniquity as wisdom. In very truth he has turned the truth of God into a lie.

Like my work at Christ's Mission, this book is intended to help both Catholics and Protestants—Catholics to arrive at the true knowledge of Christ as perfect Saviour; Protestants to encourage them to defend, at all costs, the heritage of that faith into which they were fortunately born.

May it serve, above all, to uphold Christ against everything that is not of Christ.

CHAPTER TWO

WHAT SALVATION REALLY MEANS

THE DOCTRINE OF SALVATION as I now see and experience it in Evangelical teaching, is not only different from, but diametrically opposed to what was taught to me in the Roman Catholic Church. Looking back now I am aware that, although I had no direct knowledge of what salvation really means in Christian soteriology, I was conscious of the need for something like it. I was never content with the mere half-measure of salvation which the Roman Catholic Church had to offer. There was in me a yearning, as in all men of all times, for a Saviour who really saves, and that "to the uttermost."

It was after this that my soul as a priest continually sought, and it was this unconscious longing that brought me through the historical events described in my former book, *The Soul of a Priest.*

As I see it now, in all pre-Christian religions— from the fall of man to the coming of Christ—there were two common elements: one was the need of *a priesthood of men*; the other the teaching of *an incomplete salvation.* The two were complementary of each other, since the only kind of salvation that sacrifices of men could offer must of necessity be deficient. As a result there could be no end of sin in this life, and it followed, as a consequence, that it was necessary to

believe in a further round of existences after death
wherein the still unsaved sinner would have to continue to suffer and expiate for his sins. This teaching,
in various forms, is known under the general name of
reincarnation. The Roman Catholic teaching of purgatory is but another name for this most common of
all religious teachings. To this very day, about two
thirds of the population of the world still believe in
reincarnation of one kind or another.

Now, Roman Catholicism, though it goes under
the name of the Christian religion, possesses these two
elements common to all pre-Christian religious teachings: *the need of a sacrificial priesthood,* and *incomplete salvation,* to which is added the corollary of purgatory where souls after death must suffer and expiate for sin.

So blinded was I that I was deceived into arguing
as a priest that these elements, precisely because they
were common to pre-Christian religions and Roman
Catholicism, was actual proof of their value in Christian teaching. The very antiquity of them, the fact
that they were accepted truths so long ago, is used in
Roman Catholic apologetics to prove that the Roman
Catholic Church is the only true religion. This is the
great trump argument employed against Protestantism, which Catholic apologists say dates only from the
sixteenth century.

Yet this very argument of the "oldness" of these
beliefs in Roman Catholicism is proof of their un-
Christian character. For with the coming of Jesus
Christ, the promised and long-awaited Saviour, a new
element was added to religion—one which completely

eliminated the other two. That new element is what makes Christianity unique among all religions, that makes it entirely different from all that have gone before, that makes it the only true and final religion. That new element—the "Evangel"—the "good news," is that through Christ salvation is complete. Christ our Saviour, because he is God and man, is the complete, perfect and all-sufficient mediator between God and man. Old things are passed away, and everything is made new in Him. And since the pre-Christian element of an incomplete salvation was superseded by complete salvation in Christ, the other element—a priesthood that had to offer sacrifices daily for the sins of men—must also be eliminated. This is clearly confirmed in the Epistle to the *Hebrews* (10:10-12): *"By the which we are sanctified through the offering of the body of Jesus Christ once for all . . . By a new and living way . . . Who needeth not daily, as those high priests, to offer up sacrifice, first for his own sins, and then for the people's: for this he did once, when he offered up himself." (Heb. 7: 27).*

This entirely new element of a complete and perfect work of salvation is more startling still in the fact that it makes one life on earth sufficient. He not only took away sin, but also the remembrance of it. (*Heb.* 10:2, 3). Sin therefore, in the Christian dispensation, cannot persist as something to be expiated for after death. Salvation in Christ means that you are saved completely, not half-saved; that you are made spiritually alive, not kept dead in sin. No one, in fact, can be just half-saved. To say so is a contradiction in terms.

However, Roman Catholicism is logical in offering to sinners only this in-between state of being not good enough for heaven yet not bad enough for hell when they die. In spite of its tremendous claims to be the only Church chartered by Almighty God, outside of which there is no salvation; that the pope is the infallible mouthpiece of God, is the Vicar of Jesus Christ, possessing all power in heaven and on earth, able to forgive sins and grant indulgences, to bless and to curse, and to delegate these powers to others; in spite of its wealth and grandeur as an organization, no one from the pope down to each of his ordiary priests would dare to *assure* anyone of complete salvation after one life here on earth.

It would be most inexpedient and foolish for the Church of Rome to teach otherwise. The day that the Roman Catholic Church would begin to teach the all-sufficiency of the saving work of Christ would see the end of its entire organization as now constituted. For that organization is founded upon the denial of Christ's finished work. Christ's Gospel of the "good news," with its message of full and complete salvation, would undermine the whole structure of Roman Catholicism, since it would at once dispense with the necessity of pope and priest as now ordained. It would sweep away its thinly disguised doctrine of reincarnation by making purgatory unnecessary, would rob its priests of their pretended power to offer sacrifice daily, "*first for his own sins and then for the people's,*" of being mediators between sinners and God and of forgiving them (only partially, however) of their sins in confession.

I had this proved to me some time ago when Archbishop McIntyre of New York deputed Father Richard O'Connor, professor of dogmatic theology at Dunwoodie Seminary, to approach us former priests at Christ's Mission with a proposition to induce us to return as priests to the Roman Catholic Church. Father O'Connor was a classmate of mine at the University of Propaganda Fide in Rome and I was more than happy to welcome him and to do my best to find, as he suggested, some possible common ground upon which we, as ex-priests, could meet with the doctrinal requirements of the Catholic Church and so be accepted back.

After several hours of pleasant reminiscing and discussion I put the proposition up to him in this way: "The Archbishop wants us to find a common ground upon which we might meet and be friends again. All right! Tell him that, as far as I am concerned, I will go back to the Roman Catholic Church any time he wants *on condition that I shall be allowed to believe and to preach the all sufficiency of the saving work of Christ!*" He held up his hands in horror and declared that that would be impossible!

Yet what more 'common ground' could be thought of than this most basic of all beliefs in Christian teaching! It was impossible to him because he could not logically combine this fundamental teaching of Evangelical Christianity with his sacrificial priesthood which is a standing denial of the completeness of the one sacrifice offered by Jesus Christ on Calvary. He could not admit to me the sufficiency of Christ's sacrifice offered once and forever, and then go back

and teach a denial of this to his class of students for
the priesthood in the seminary that turns out priests
by the hundred for the Archdiocese of New York.

How the Catholic Church advertises itself as being able to make up for the deficiency in Christ's saving work may be seen from any of its many newspapers and periodicals. *Our Sunday Visitor,* popular
weekly Catholic paper that is sold at Catholic
Churches on Sundays throughout the country, in its
issue for October 4, 1942, claimed that indulgences
and masses can be paid to the Almighty for the souls
in purgatory "just as I can pay the bill you owe to
your butcher or to your grocer." Here are its exact
words:

*"Most Indulgences are applicable to the souls in
purgatory, who cannot help themselves, but who can
be helped by the suffrages (especially masses) of
friends on earth, as well as by the indulgences gained
in their behalf. Just as I can pay the bill you owe to
your butcher or to your grocer, so I can apply to the
debt still owed to Almighty God by a soul in purgatory
the prayers and good works I perform."*

This makes big business, in money and work, for
the priests, and would be impossible if they were to
teach that Christ has paid all the debt by his shed
blood on Calvary.

It is no wonder then that the decrees of the Council of Trent anathematized (cursed) all who would
dare to say that sinners are completely justified by
Christ's saving grace alone. Here are some of these
Canons of the Council of Trent and their anathemas:

Canon IX: "If anyone says that by faith alone the sinner is justified, so that no cooperation is required on his part in order to obtain the grace of justification, and that it is not necessary that he be prepared and disposed by the movement of his own will; let him be accursed."

Canon X: "If anyone says that men are justified, either by the sole imputation of the justice of Christ or by the sole remission of sins, to the exclusion of the grace and charity which is poured forth in their hearts by the Holy Ghost and is inherent in them; or even that the grace, whereby we are justified, is solely the favor of God; let him be accursed."

Canon XII: "If anyone says that justifying faith is nothing else but confidence in the divine mercy which remits sin for Christ's sake; or that this confidence alone is that whereby we are justified; let him be accursed."

Canon XIII: "If anyone says that it is necessary for everyone in order to obtain the remission of sins, that he believe for certain, and without any wavering arising from his own infirmity and indisposition, that his sins are forgiven him; let him be accursed."

Canon XIV: "If anyone says that man is truly absolved from his sins and justified because he assuredly believes himself absolved and justified; or that no one is truly justified but he who believes himself justified; let him be accursed."

One of the six most deadly sins against the Holy Spirit listed in the Roman Catholic (Baltimore) Catechism is: *"Presumption of being saved without merits."* This mortal sin of presumption is basic to the whole teaching of Roman Catholic soteriology. If Roman Catholic people were taught by their priests

that sinners are fully justified and saved by the imputation of the justice of Christ, the sacrifice of the
mass, purgatory, indulgences and the host of other
Roman Catholic beliefs and practices upon which the
structure of Roman Catholicism rests, would automatically cease to exist.

CHAPTER THREE

HOW SINS ARE REALLY FORGIVEN

IF I WERE ASKED to point out the fundamental fault in the Roman Catholic Church, I would say: *its very success as a popular religion.* For, in order to make itself and its teachings popular, to become the great religio-political machine that it is, it has been forced to bring the things of God down to the attractive level of the human heart. The price it has had to pay for its success in accomplishing this is the whittling down of the truth of God—the actual *"turning of the truth of God into a lie."* (*Rom.* 1: 25).

Since my conversion I have studied somewhat the writings and motives of the great priest-reformers of the Protestant Reformation period—Luther, Knox, Calvin, Wycliffe, and others. These have confirmed my own findings that the glaring fault of Roman Catholicism is its treatment of the truth of God as truth is treated among men in worldly dealings with one another in their business and political relations. Unmindful of Christ's warning, the Roman Catholic Church is not only *in* the world but *of* it. Everyone knows that in business advertisements, legal affairs and political diplomacy words are used chiefly to hide the truth, or at best to express half-truths. To apply words in this way to explain and teach the truth of

our redemption robs Christian faith and morals of
their whole worth and meaning.

Nowhere is this seen at its worst than in Roman
Catholicism's moral code. Here the framework used is
the old law and penal system of imperial Rome, with
its obligations by contract and delict, its view of in-
curring debts and the modes of extinguishing and
transmuting them. Into this framework the Church of
Rome has fitted the ten commandments of God and
added other commandments of its own. The result is
a moral code that is mostly concerned about ways
and means by which sins may be committed or sidestepped without actually breaking the commandments
of God.

Sin is basic in all religious systems, and the system that can autocratically control, forgive (partially) and multiply sins, attains greatest power over
the people. Here at once can be seen again the chasm
that divides pre-Christian religions and their present-
day imitators from true Christian teaching. The former could not, even if they wanted, "with those
sacrifices which they offered year by year continually,
make the comers thereunto perfect," as the *Epistle
to the Hebrews* (10:1) tells us. The reason for this is
clearly stated in the next verse of this same Epistle:
*"For then would they not have ceased to be offered?
Because the worshippers once purged, would have had
no more conscience of sins. For in those sacrifices there
is a remembrance again made of sins ..."*

In other words, pre-Christian religions—and the
Roman Catholic Church which insists on daily sacrifices—had the effect of keeping people in sin and in

remembrance of it, of even increasing it. This gave them great power, for everyone had to look to their priests to obtain whatever temporary surcease from sin that was offered. True Christianity, that is, Christ's one and all-sufficient sacrifice, cleanses the sinner completely from all sin, and from even the remembrance of it in the conscience. Furthermore, the power and glory that results from this redounds to no human being or religious corporation, but to Christ alone.

In the Roman Catholic Church the handling of sin is arranged in such a way that everything done for sinners redounds to the power and prestige of the Church and its priests. By its treatment of sin on the human level it makes itself a very popular religion and appeals, not only to the natural weaknesses in its own multitude of followers, but also to the vaster number of the unchurched and unbelievers who in their daily lives are affected by its moral code, especially in the large centers of population in America where Roman Catholics (and sin) abound. Roman Catholic Bishop John F. Noll of Ft. Wayne, Indiana, speaking before the National Catholic Conference on Family Life in Chicago on March 12, 1947, was reported by the N. Y. *Times* as publicly confirming this when he admitted that: *"Nearly all the evils of society prevail most where we* (Catholics) *live and not where Protestants live."*

Although it may seem harsh for me to say so, the fact cannot be denied that the chief business of the Roman Catholic Church is to see to it that sin remains and is even increased among men. In the first place, it does not, and cannot, offer complete salvation from sin. In the second place, if it preached the complete abolition of sin by Christ's sacrifice once offered, it would be forced to discontinue the sacrifices of the mass daily offered by its priests. For the one and all-sufficient sacrifice of Christ on Calvary, as the New Testament teaches, purges the conscience of sin and the very remembrance of it. On the other hand, in the sacrifices of Roman Catholic priests, like the sacrifices of pre-Christian religions, *"there is remembrance again made of sin,"* neither can they, like the sacrifices of old, *"make the comers thereunto perfect."*

It should not be surprising, therefore, to find that the Roman Catholic Church actually fosters and specializes in sin. Its moral code consists mainly in a set of legalisms that multiplies sins by distinctions and divisions, thus creating many ways of committing sin. The corollary of this is that ways and means must at once be found to make it easy to forgive the multitude of sins thus created. The Jesuits, the ruling caste of priests in the Catholic Church, have specialized in this. Their system of 'probabilism,' now almost universally accepted by other priests in their practice of the confessional, consists in finding as many reasons as possible for granting absolution to sinners. They accept mere remorse, or pure fear of hell, as sufficient substitute for true repentance. They go to the extreme of granting forgiveness even if the penitent admits that he is *merely sorry because he can't be sorry* for his sins.

A practical example of this may be seen in the Catholic-propaganda novel, *The World, the Flesh and*

Father Smith, by Bruce Marshall, a best-seller and selection of the Book-of-the-Month Club.[1] On pages 16 to 22, the author describes how Father Smith, a very humane and zealous priest, forgives the sins of a dying sailor in a house of prostitution: "He started off to tell the priest about all the women he had known in Buenos Aires and Hong Kong and said that he had liked the women in Hong Kong best." When the priest rebuked him for talking this way on his deathbed about the "tawdry Jezebels in foreign ports," the dying sailor spoke back and said "the women weren't tawdry at all especially the ones in China, who had gold on their fingernails and wore black satin slippers with high red heels, and that now that he came to think of it *he wasn't sorry for having known all these women at all, since they had all been so beautiful and that he would like to know them again if he got the chance*."

The old sailor had only a few minutes to live, so the author describes the priest as applying the Jesuit principle of 'probabilism' in the following way:
"In despair Father Smith asked the old sailor *if he was sorry for not being sorry* for having known all these women, and the old sailor said that *yes he was sorry for not being sorry*. Whereupon Father Smith said that he thought God would understand, and *he absolved the old sailor from his sins*, pouring the merits of Christ's passion over the old sailor's forgetfulness of God and those long-ago dresses that had made such lovely sounds."

---

[1] Houghton Mifflin Co., 1945.

Many Protestants, and many more who profess no religion, considered this a very 'human' and realistic story, and, as a best-seller book, it added more grist to the Catholic propaganda mill. They were entirely oblivious of the absurdity—the blasphemy, I should say—of making it appear that a priest had the power "to pour the merits of Christ's Passion" over a hardened and clearly unrepentant sinner, just because by the trick words of a phrase he satisfied the requirements of sophistic theologians.

There are four main divisions of sin in Roman Catholic teaching: 1. *Original sin,* which is taken away only by Baptism, and without which there is no possibility at all of getting to heaven; 2. *Mortal sin,* which must be confessed in every detail to a priest; 3. *Venial sin,* which need not be confessed and which may be taken away by penances or other means; 4. *Sins against Church laws,* which in turn may be either mortal or venial.

The Catholic moral theologians keep close watch on all classifications and divisions of sins and often add new ones. They become specialists in sin. Mortal sin is "deadly" and unless a person in mortal sin is forgiven by a priest before he dies he goes to hell. But even if he obtains this pardon, a large but unknown amount of punishment remains to be expiated for in purgatory. Non-mortal sins need not be confessed to a priest, but generally it is safer to do so, since the priest alone is the judge of what sins are mortal or merely venial.

The amount of money one may steal without committing a mortal sin depends upon the economic levels in different countries or sections of a country. Only recently it has been laid down that in the United States one may steal up to $40.00 without committing a mortal sin.[2] Drinking, gambling and other habits considered as vices by Protestants are not counted as evil at all except when indulged in to excess—the point of excess being left to the priest in confession to determine.

Specious ways are found by which one may break the ten commandments without committing sin. If one is in extreme need of something, he may steal it from another if by so doing he does not reduce the other person to his state of need. Likewise, one may secretly compensate oneself for services or goods to which he considers he has a right.[3] Some of the most deadly sins are those against the Catholic Church's own commandments, such as missing mass on Sunday and eating meat on Friday. Joining in prayer with a Protestant and, in some places, even entering a Protestant church, is a mortal sin. It is much more difficult, for instance, for a priest to obtain pardon of his sin of getting legally married than to get absolution for the crime of murder.

This expedient regulating of sin and vice appeals especially to those who are not members of the Roman Catholic Church. It is very profitable for those engaged in the liquor business, in gambling and other vices.

---

[2] For photographic proof of this, see, *The Secret of Catholic Power*, by L. H. Lehmann, Agora Publishing Company.

[3] These *"Reasons that excuse from theft,"* are listed in *The Manual of Christian Doctrine*, page 279, a catechism for use in Catholic schools and colleges and officially endorsed by the highest Roman Catholic authorities.

It appeals to the weaknesses of human nature in all men. Above all, it secures the Catholic Church's power over great multitudes of men, in this life and the next.

Diametrically opposed to this expedient regulating of sin and vice for power purposes, is the treatment of sin as I have discovered it in the new dispensation of Evangelical Christianity. Sin now can be taken away *in toto*, not by any weekly 'laundering' process of the soul in confession to a priest, but by the gift of a whole new soul. This new process is as far apart from the expedient human level of the Roman Catholic method of absolution as heaven is from earth.

No man or organization, but God, can get glory from it, since it is His gift, the finished product of His hand. It fully takes away sin, and therefore leaves no opportunity to the religion that teaches it to build up power over men by keeping them continually in sin, or, at best, only half-forgiven. The religion that teaches it cannot become corrupt, since it does not lend itself to any compromise with politicians, the liquor business or the gambling interests. It makes those who teach it and those who are taught equal, since all share in the common priesthood of believers, and all have the same need of it; in effect it works equally in all. But the religion that teaches it in its fullness will never be popular as the Roman Catholic religion is, nor as attractive to the multitudes as the moral code of the Church of Rome will always remain, as long as the heart of man remains unregenerate.

Here is a summary contrasting the two:

Roman Catholicism teaches:

1. The necessity of a sacrificial priesthood;
2. Incomplete Salvation;
3. You cannot escape sin, even after death. Your only hope is in the Church, which controls sin but cannot assure you of complete pardon.

Evangelical Christianity teaches:

1. The priesthood of all believers, and the high priesthood of Christ alone;
2. Complete and full salvation in Christ;
3. Sin is sin, and the only absolution from sin is through a whole New Life in Christ.

CHAPTER FOUR

COUNTERFEIT CHRISTIANITY

BECAUSE two things outwardly look alike is no proof that they are identical. For one of the oldest tricks known to man is by false appearance to make a worthless thing look genuine. Often, in fact, the greater the apparent similarity, the greater the real difference beneath the surface. Despite a perfect likeness, counterfeit money hasn't even one cent of real value.

It should not be surprising then to find that men have counterfeited the religion of Jesus Christ to make it serve the evil ends of arbitrary power and oppression. Obviously evil would not be accepted, were it to appear as evil; it is therefore disguised as good. Falsehood would be rejected if it were not made to look like the truth. No one would deal with the devil as such; accordingly he takes on the appearance of his direct opposite—of God himself. To discover those who destroy true Christian teaching, you must look behind the banner of Christ they brazenly flourish. In this way you can expect to find the Antichrist usurping the place of Christ and appearing as the leader of all Christian people. He will naturally give the impression of being entirely *for*, not *against* Christ; for "anti," the prefix in his name, means 'taking the place of,' or 'usurping'—that is, he appears as the 'vicar' of Christ.

Judged by this test the Church of Rome can be seen in its true light. It puts a pope in the place of Christ, and substitutes his dictatorial word for the Word of God. It emphasizes Mary for Jesus, and a dead image on a crucifix for a living, triumphant Saviour in the hearts of men. In the words of Cardinal Newman: "It substitutes external ritual for moral obedience, penance for penitence, confession for sorrow, profession for faith, the lips for the heart." Its 'Vicar of Christ' wears a triple crown, flaunts proud titles and surrounds himself with the trappings of the Roman Caesars, dispenses Christian justice by the law code of pagan Rome, rushes to ally himself with oppressors of the people, depends on politics rather than prayer.

How best to expose this counterfeit of Christianity is the problem that I have worked on for the past ten years as director of Christ's Mission in New York and editor of *The Converted Catholic Magazine.* We live in an age of extreme tolerance as far as religious beliefs are concerned, and since my conversion I have become a citizen of the United States which has risked its very existence, the lives of its young men and spent astronomical amounts of its money in two world wars in the fight for the preservation of the right of everyone to find, to teach and believe about God and salvation according to the dictates of his own conscience. All the hopes and aspirations of this great democratic nation are irrevocably tied to defense of these principles of freedom—religious, political and social.

For this reason, there are many who are opposed to anything being said or done against any Church or

religious organization, no matter how corrupt it may
be. Others say that in criticizing or taking any action
against a corrupt religious organization such as the
Roman Catholic Church we should be always 'constructive,' never 'destructive' in our methods. They
speak as if nothing is ever so bad that it could not be
set right again by the application of certain correc-
tives and palliatives, by a few patches here and there,
and a new coat of paint to make it look brand new
again.

Yet it would be both foolish and dangerous to
patch up in this way, and paint a house or other build-
ing that is decayed from its very foundations. Jesus
Christ warned against the uselessness of putting a new
patch on an old worn-out garment, and against the
danger of putting new wine into old bottles. Both the
new and the old suffer destruction in the end. Often
those who want only 'constructive' criticism of an institution do not want any criticism at all. Totally destructive criticism is necessary if the occasion calls for
it. How, for instance, can one be 'constructively' criti-
cal of the devil and his works?

It is well to remember God's commission to the
prophet Jeremiah (*Jer.* 1:10): *"I have this day set
thee over the nations and over the kingdoms, to root
out, and to pull down, to overthrow and to destroy,
to build and to plant."* Here God's order is to do six
things, the first four of which are destructive—to
root out, pull down, overthrow and destroy—and then
—to build and to plant.

I have come to the conclusion that this 'destructive' method is necessary when occasions call for it,

in the case of decayed religious institutions as well as of decayed buildings. In order for the seed of the Gospel of Jesus Christ to take root in the hearts of men, they must first be purged and cleansed of all the superstitious, pagan teachings with which they have been poisoned by the false teachings and practices of the Roman Church. A strong spiritual emetic is needed for this purpose.

In collaboration with others at Christ's Mission who have also been converted from the Roman Catholic priesthood, I have in these past ten years tried to make up for "the years that the locust hath eaten," when I blindly taught the errors I now fight against. I have done so in a fair, factual and objective manner, and in a spirit of love toward the Roman Catholic people who are of my own household. The spiritual emetic that we offer them is strong, so strong that it makes many sick before it makes them well. That emetic is the full and unabridged Gospel message of salvation through personal acceptance of Jesus Christ.

I realize how difficult it is for Roman Catholics to accept and believe this true Christian message of salvation. It cannot be forcibly thrust upon them. It is such strong meat for them that they often will vomit it back immediately. It seems too terrifying for them to believe all at once that their powerful and grandiose Church organization that has lasted all through the centuries could be false or deceptive. Protestant teaching about salvation, they say, is too simple, too negative; it has no signs of power; it does nothing to act upon you by means of ritual or priestly ministrations. It is a sin of presumption, they say, to believe that God will save you completely in one life, and piously and humbly say they are not worthy to enter heaven immediately after they die. They are fearful of throwing away the useless burden of superstitious beliefs in the mediatorship of Mary, the saints and their devotions and images and, trusting entirely in the sacrifice of Christ once offered, follow boldly after him entirely naked of these pagan practices and beliefs foisted upon them by a power-seeking priesthood.

Many think us enemies of God, betrayers of Jesus Christ as Judas was. The character of the ex-priest has been so blackened by calumnies since Luther's time, that the unsuspecting Catholic people, if they allow their minds at all to admit that priests do leave the Church, unconsciously look upon us as completely lost souls working in the devil's behalf. Yet tens of thousands of Roman Catholic people leave the Roman Catholic Church each year and affiliate with the Protestant denominations. Several hundred former priests have been helped, both spiritually and economically, through Christ's Mission since its founding in 1879 by Father James A. O'Connor.

I am convinced that there are only two courses open to the Roman Catholic Church: either a thorough reform of itself from within, or total disruption from without. In helping both, I consider my present work constructively advantageous not only in the cause of Christ, but in the spiritual interests of my former Roman Catholic people.

Chapter Five

RELIGION AS A SYSTEM OF POWER

RELIGION can uplift its devotees only if its worship is upward, if the image and object of its devotion are above the level of man. It is an historic fact that religions which have descended to the deification of creatures, whether of men or animals, have degraded, enslaved and impoverished their believers.

It would seem that those who controlled such religions purposely established their worship downward. They focussed the attention of their people on glorified snakes, sacred symbols, bread and wine, and on pictures and statues of men and women with haloes around their heads. The purpose of this was not to allow the common man a vision of anything above him that was not more exalted than the hierarchical priesthood in power over him. Above all, the worshipper was never allowed to contact directly and rise to the exalted plane of God. For if this had been allowed, then the priests of those religions would have been exposed for what they were—mere men wrapped in a nebulous cloak of sanctity.

With the exception of the religion of the Jews, all pre-Christian religions imaged their Gods and focussed their worship on or below the level of human nature. Even the Jews at times were led by their priests to descend to the worship of snakes and bulls. But not even the Jewish religion could make it known that the common man could actually become a partaker of the very nature of God, and thus change his slave relation, to God and man, for one of rightful sonship of God.

Of particular significance is the fact that the female form of a Goddess was used—as it is today in big-business advertising—as the greatest attraction to the worshippers of all pre-Christian pagan religions. The names of such Goddesses are as numerous as the religions of which they were made the top-ranking attraction: Aphrodite, Astarte, Venus, Ishtar, Ashtaroth, Lakmi, Freia, Mylitta, Kypris, Isis, and a host of others. Even the highest God of such religions was dwarfed into insignificance by the female form of the Goddesses. It may have been that, in the beginning, a more or less high concept of God was worshipped in these religions. But eventually they all ended up by the image of that God as a tiny, helpless babe on the breast of the Goddess.

All pagan religions have developed in this way. The end-product of this paganization of religion can always be seen by this phenomenon of God as a help-less, suckling babe at a woman's breast. The creature is exalted and God is debased. I have scarcely any need to call attention to the sad fact that this is what has also happened in the religious teaching and wor-ship of the Church of Rome. Mary, as the Madonna who is worshipped under countless different names in the Roman Catholic Church, has been magnified, as Astarte, Venus, Isis and the other pagan Goddesses, above Christ. In all the various forms her statues take in Roman Catholic Churches, Christ is minimized to the form of a tiny, helpless babe on her breast. Mary is made, in Roman Catholic teaching, the "Mediatrix of all graces." No one can get to God or her son Jesus except through her. How different from the Mary of Scripture who, in her song the *Magnificat*, humbly declares in unison with all sinners: *"My soul doth magnify the Lord; my spirit hath rejoiced in God my Saviour."* (*Luke* 1: 46, 47).

It is then but another short step to apply to Mary the offices and titles that belong exclusively to Jesus Christ. Thus she is called "The Gate of Heaven," "Mother of Mercy." In the most common of all Roman Catholic prayers, the *"Hail, Holy Queen,"* Mary is fervently beseeched as: "Our Life, Our Sweetness and Our Hope!"

Only in true Christian teaching is the sinner offered actual sonship of God and encouraged to become a partaker in the very nature of God Himself. This most exalted of religious concepts, whereby each individual is liberated from the power of priests and tyrannical overlords and made a rightful heir of God, is alone the heritage of the Christian religion. It puts an end to the need of human mediatorship—of priests and Goddesses, of glorified snakes and other animals, and points the soul to Christ as the one and all-sufficient mediator and Saviour.

To me who came to the light of this glorious message only after many years of wasted effort as a priest, it appears as the greatest tragedy of all human history that this teaching was betrayed by those who actually set themselves up as the supreme and infallible hierarchs of the Christian Church. And behind this betrayal was the lust for power, a power over men and nations built upon the most sacred instinct

in the hearts of all men—the yearning for a true
Saviour. The popes of Rome have gone so far in as-
suming the power of God that they insist on being
called "the Holy Father," the name used by Jesus
Christ for Almighty God alone.

I know well the excuse that is made to try and
justify this assumption of power and the exclusive
monopoly of the things of God by the priesthood of
the Roman Catholic Church. They say that exalted
teaching and upward worship are beyond the reach of
the common man, that the masses of ignorant and
crude people they minister to are not capable of understanding anything unless it is presented to them in
the "grosser vessel" of human nature. What they really
mean is that the easiest and most successful way to
obtain unlimited control over the people is to legislate
about heaven, hell and purgatory through their weak
passions.

This may have been justified to a certain extent
in the pagan religions of pre-Christian times, when
there was no real Saviour available, and when a few
favored 'mystics' allocated to themselves the knowledge of the inner secrets of God. But Jesus Christ
taught no "lesser vehicle" with inner secrets for a
favored few. He chose his apostles from the broad
masses of the poor, working-class people. He was the
great democratic revolutionist in religion. He opened
the flood-gates of God's power upon all the people.
The millennial effects of this religious revolution will
be felt only when all the people are allowed to know
the whole truth and experience the full power of God
through Christ our Saviour.

CHAPTER SIX

FALSE LOYALTY

When treason's truth, and loyal is falsely true ...

MY REPUDIATION of the Roman Catholic priesthood was primarily an effort to preserve self-integrity. It called for disloyality to a grandiose institution for selfish reasons. For I am convinced that in spiritual matters one must be selfish, since salvation is necessarily something solely between the individual soul and God.

It has been well said that many will not hesitate to compromise the things of God for the sake of an institution, but few will compromise an institution for the sake of God. That is the choice before a priest when he discovers that his Church organization is an obstacle to his spiritual welfare. For absolute loyalty to the organization is a requisite for salvation in the Roman Catholic Church.

This is not the case, however, with Protestant clergymen, since a Protestant minister may oppose his Church organization without jeopardizing his soul's salvation. He may change to another denomination without loss even of social prestige or economic standing, or he may continue to preach the Gospel without membership in any Church institution whatever.

There come times in the life of everyone when it is treasonable to be truthful, and to be loyal is to be falsely true. This is especially the case with many otherwise honest priests of the Catholic Church. They consider themselves irrevocably tied to an organization that they believed at first to possess the only way of salvation for themselves and the whole world. By the time they become aware of the deception practiced upon them, they say it is too late and too difficult to leave it. To remain within the organization and admit the deception, they say, is like being disloyal to the mother that bore you, or to be like an officer of a bank who, knowing the bank is crooked, warns depositors to withdraw their money from it. Thus they remain loyal to the Church and become untrue to themselves.

St. Paul (1 *Tim.* 4: 2) warns against those *"speaking lies in hypocrisy; having their conscience seared with a hot iron,"* thus depriving it of the power of making proper moral decisions.

I feel sad to think of the many priests I have known in the Roman Catholic Church who have allowed their conscience to be thus 'cauterized' as the only way of being able to continue to teach and preach what they no longer fully believe. Many otherwise honest priests come to the parting of the ways with their Church for conscience sake, but turn back for fear of being termed disloyal. To remain contented thereafter they must suffer this cauterizing of their conscience.

It was against this crime in the theological system of the Roman Catholic Church that the priest-reformers of the sixteenth century particularly protested. The demand they made for reformation was primarily a moral one. They were convinced that the teaching and practices of the Church of Rome were not in accord with the moral law of God, and that they could not, in conscience, continue to abide by them. They knew, as I came to realize, that to be content with such teachings involved consent to have one's conscience seared and robbed by the theologians of its right to discern between truth and lying, between honesty and fraud.

The *theologian* has his place in religion, but his task is limited to instructing us in matters of doctrine, discipline and worship. The *scholar*, too, has his place in religion, which is to help us understand obscure sayings and difficult problems. But the really important factor in religion is the individual *conscience*.

In the Roman Catholic Church the theologian has usurped all three of these, and the result has been, on the one hand, the stultification of the moral conscience in the Roman Catholic people, and on the other, the twisting of the Christian moral code by the theologians to serve the power and organization of the Church. Thomas Carlyle, famous British author, has well said that the Jesuits have *"poisoned the wellsprings of truth."* More horrifying still is the "moral theology" of Alphonsus Liguori, who is counted a saint and a "doctor" of the Church—of equal rank with Augustine, Chrysostom and others—whose textbooks are standard on moral questions in all Roman Catholic seminaries. The "moral" teachings of

Liguori, if they could be read in their original Latin, would fill every right-minded person with horror. For there he outlines *the ways in which falsehood can be used without really telling a lie; the ways in which the property of others can be taken without stealing; how the ten commandments can be broken without committing deadly sin.* No one should wonder, then, that the proportion of Roman Catholic criminals in our jails and penitentiaries, and juvenile delinquents, far exceeds the percentage of Roman Catholics in the general population of the United States.

This important matter of the treatment of the conscience creates another pivotal point of difference between Roman Catholicism and Protestantism in religious affairs, and between fascism and democracy in governmental matters. When a theological system goes out of its domain and assumes to itself even the consciences of men, it sets up a religious totalitarianism. Mussolini, Hitler and the other fascist dictators did this same thing. They took away the right of the individual to follow his own conscience as to right and wrong in matters of government and made the "leader," the *Fuehrer, Duce, Caudillo,* the sole arbiter of right and wrong. By restoring the conscience to the individual, the Protestant Reformation not only checked the abuse of spiritual totalitarianism in the Church, but also established the right of the individual to democratic freedoms in the State.

William L. Sullivan, the Irish-American priest of the Paulist order, who left the Catholic Church, in his book, *Under Orders,* traces the whole failure of Roman Catholicism as a Christian Church to its abandonment of the moral law and the fabrication by its theologians of *"moulds and forms that do violence in a man's inmost life, and which constitute an irksome artifice which falsifies him, rather than a joyous guidance which develops and fulfills him."* He saw that the moral law of God "required of me that I should see evil as evil everywhere and in whomsoever, without respect of persons of station," and that evil does not cease to be evil when sprinkled with theological perfume.

Power and success have come to the Roman Catholic Church as a result of this stultification of the individual conscience and the fabrication of moulds and forms that do violence to man's inner life. Many Protestant ministers foolishly envy its authoritarian discipline, forgetful of the fact that this has been attained at the cost of the betrayal of Christianity's true code of morals. Not only can true Christian teaching co-exist with imperfect Church discipline and democratic organizational form, but I think they are essential to it.

CHAPTER SEVEN

NEW CREATION IN CHRIST

"By the works of the law no flesh shall be justified in his sight, for by the law is the knowledge of sin."
(Rom. 3: 20).

THE CONFLICT between Roman Catholicism and Protestantism centers around the opposing teachings of salvation by faith and salvation by works. Protestantism, which is the reassertion of the original Gospel teaching of Christianity, insists with the Apostle Paul that works according to the law in the spiritual life not only do not justify, but are the cause of sin and condemnation: "The law was given to condemn, not to justify" (*Rom.* 3: 19). Again to *Titus* (3: 5) Paul lays it down that *"Not by works of righteousness which we have done, but according to his mercy he saved us, by the washing of regeneration, and the renewing of the Holy Ghost."* Roman Catholicism continues the pre-Christian religious teaching that for eternal salvation it is necessary to carry out to the letter the laws laid down by the theologians and priests of the Church.

This does not mean, as Catholic people are falsely told by their priests, that Protestants teach that, as long as you believe, you can sin as you like. This is a calumny on Protestants. Their teaching is that good

works are not the *cause* but the *effect* of our salvation,
that salvation means *a new creation in Christ Jesus,*
that it is a *free gift,* that good works come not before
but *follow after* regeneration which can only be accomplished by faith in Christ: *"For we are his workmanship, created in Christ Jesus unto good works,
which God hath before ordained that we should walk
in them"* (*Ephes.* 2: 10). There can be no good works
in the spiritual order before the new birth, since the
only work that God will call good is the work that is
brought forth by the power of the indwelling Christ
—*"Christ in you both to will and to do."*

If you go to Tibet you will find along the banks
of the rivers groups of men holding in their hands
long poles with strings dangling from them over the
water. They sit there day after day lifting and drop-
ping the poles. At first glance it would seem as if they
were fishing. On closer examination, however, you will
find that there is a weight at the end of the string, and
on the weight is an engraving of Buddha. All day long
they raise and lower their poles, letting the weight
splash upon the surface of the river. Ask them what
they are doing and they will reply: "Storing up merit." The larger the number of impressions they make
with the image on the water the greater will be their
merit with God after they die!

Yet this is identical with the teaching of the
Roman Catholic Church under the name of Christianity. Like the heathen who have never heard of the
name of Christ, Catholics are also taught that it is
necessary to "earn" their salvation by repeated human acts, and that excess merit, resulting from mass-

es, fastings, rosaries, medals, scapulars and repetition of prayer formulas, is "stored up" for them in heaven.

Here we have illustrated the "bondage of doing," of substituting human actions—which often have no value even in human life—for the accomplishing of something altogether beyond the power of man himself. This is the bondage in which the Church of Rome keeps its millions of adherents. It is not only un-Christian but unjust and dishonest.

A Buddhist believer, for instance, who is less pious than others may be able to afford a better and longer fishing pole, may be more expert than his more pious brethren in casting the image of Buddha upon the surface of the water, and would therefore store up more merit than the others. So also in the Church of Rome the poor and the ignorant are at a disadvantage. Those with money can have masses offered for themselves which the poor cannot afford. Those with education and higher intelligence can study to know the fine points of the laws of the Church, upon which eternal salvation or damnation is believed to depend.

What if one Roman Catholic more pious than the rest should fail in the knowledge of some necessary requirement of the law? In all religions that profess to dispense grace according to works of ecclesiastical laws, new requirements are constantly added to such an extent that the mass of ordinary believers cannot fail to be in ignorance of the latest additions to them. The Church of Rome makes no allowance for ignorance of the laws it makes and upon which the salvation of souls is made to depend. Its canon law, identical with the harsh rule of ancient Rome, lays it down as a basic principle that "ignorance of the law does not excuse" (*Ignorantia legis non excusat*).

Where is the pity for those who want to do all that is necessary but fail because they have not learned of some last requirement? Where is that equality before God, which is basic in Christian teaching, in a system that affords its priests opportunity to study the law, to offer masses for themselves without cost, and which dispenses to the rich spiritual benefits denied to the poor because they cannot afford to pay for them?

God is to be thanked that I am now free of all this to preach and teach that above the woe and the sin, the evil and the failure of men, there stands the cross of Christ with its power to save all "to the uttermost." Against the darkness of heathenism and the futility of human works to save it stands written: *"Believe on the Lord Jesus Christ and thou shalt be saved!"*

CHAPTER EIGHT

CHRIST JESUS—AS SOVEREIGN LORD

"O Foolish Galatians, who hath bewitched you . . ."
(Gal. 3:1).

SACERDOTALISM concerns itself chiefly with the sphere of nature, with things of the natural heart, and in keeping the gaze of its devotees down to things of earth. It appeals to man's aversion to spiritual worship and panders to his propensity for the 'miraculous' by means of what St. Paul calls the "beggarly elements" (*Gal.* 4:10).

A hierarchical priesthood must have a *victim*, over which it can exercise control and which must never be able to either fully redeem or wholly mediate. Its aim is to develop natural devotion, never a spiritual relationship by which its devotees will renounce priestly power and pay homage to a higher being as sovereign Lord.

Excuses may be made for priesthoods in pre-Christian times. For then there was no way by which man could rise to full personal spiritual relationship with God. In Christ Jesus, however, mankind now has not only a complete redeemer and saviour, but also a glorified sovereign Lord. *"God hath made that same Jesus whom ye have crucified both Lord and Christ."* (*Acts* 2:36). He, once the humbled victim on the cross, is now sovereign Lord and the head and authority of every man.

The Roman Catholic priesthood, true to its traditional role of deceiving by half-measures, has taken the humbled and crucified Jesus for its *victim*, to the exclusion of the Christ as glorified sovereign Lord and Master. Over this victim, Jesus in the flesh, Roman priests claim to exercise all the control of pagan priesthoods over their helpless and fleshly victims. This devotion to a dead, humbled and conquered Jesus, unless it is transformed into a spiritual relationship, results in the ultimate denial of Jesus as sovereign Lord. Thus, Roman Catholic priests are deputed to "sacrifice" him every day, to dissect and portion him out to their people, to limit his power, and to make sure that their followers will never be taught to look to him as reigning in power above all men.

This purely bodily relationship that is stressed by the Roman Catholic priesthood leads to the absurd extreme of actually carving up the body of Jesus Christ into different parts, for special fleshly devotions. Thus his heart is taken out, enlarged, and set up as a distinct object of worship and adoration. In like manner his face, his five wounds, his blood, even his crown of thorns, are set apart from the rest of his body and particular novenas and devotions established in their honor. The descent is short and sudden to such pietistic absurdities as "Most Sacred Heart!" "O Adorable Face!" "Most Precious Blood!" Orders of nuns and monks, even schools and colleges, are named after these dissected parts of the body of Jesus, and such crowning absurdities as the following often appear in the sports pages of our newspapers: *"Sacred Heart beats Holy Cross!"*

This refined irreverence of sentimental devotions tends to spiritual vanity and corruption. The very name of Jesus is brought down to the level of an indulgent human nature. His immutable holiness is darkened by the obvious implication that *he will overlook and let offenses remain.* He himself is pictured as someone that men *approve* of. They are taught to call him "O Sweetest Jesus!" "O Amiable Jesus!" as if he were an *"agreeable," "goodnatured"* person, according to the dictionary meaning of the words. It all tends, on the one hand, to sap his spiritual power, and on the other, to give priests more power over him, to handle him as they do other pious objects, to divide him up into convenient parts—a power even to mishandle, insult and degrade him, as is sometimes done in Roman Catholic countries with the wafer of bread that is supposed to be the very flesh and blood of Jesus Christ.[1]

The latest attempt to diminish the saving power of Jesus Christ is contained in a Jesuit booklet which claims that the "sacrifice" of the mass offered by Roman Catholic priests is not only *equal* to the sacrifice of Calvary, but even *"adds"* something more to it; that it even *"improves"* on Calvary.[2]

To bring their helpless victim Jesus Christ down farther still on the human level, they identify him with mere creatures. Thus the popular Roman Catholic ejaculation *"Jesus, Mary, Joseph!"* To Mary are

[1] I refer here to the *"Black Mass"* and demon worship, in which the power of Satan is conjured up by horrible misuse of the communion wafer.

[2] See, *My Mind Wanders*, by Jesuit Father John P. Delaney (p. 15) and *officially endorsed by Cardinal Spellman of New York*, and his ecclesiastical censors.

attributed all the offices that belong alone to Christ Jesus. She is prayed to as *"Our Way," "Our Hope," "Our Life."* The pope is now planning to decree, as a dogma of eternal truth to be believed under threat of eternal damnation, that Mary, like Jesus, was also taken up bodily into heaven.

All of which is obviously Satan's plan eventually to have the creature Mary as a goddess supplant entirely the Son of God, Christ Jesus our Lord. *Satan's triumph over the Christian religion will be complete when the Lord of Glory becomes the effeminate offspring of a goddess in the minds of his creatures. All paganisms have developed in this way.*

True Christians express their reverence, declare their allegiance and testify to the Lordship of Christ Jesus by the way in which they approach him. They reflect the Scriptures in this regard and refer to the risen Christ always as *Lord*. A light, unreserved use of his personal name indicates at best a fragmentary conception of Jesus, the sovereign Lord.

The Gospel of *John* (12:41) records that when Isaiah beheld the glory of the *"High and lofty One that inhabiteth eternity, whose name is Holy"* (*Isa.* 57:16), he spoke of Jesus. Before him the seraphim with veiled faces ever proclaim his holiness. And it is at the name of Jesus, the pre-announced name under which he bore the sins of the world, the name above every name, that every one shall eventually bow and confess his Lordship. How infinitely glorious is that name!

CHAPTER NINE

THE IMPOSSIBILITY OF PURGATORY

THE WHOLE KEY to the "new message"—the Evangel—of Christian teaching is its assurance of an immediate state of felicity after death for believers on the Lord Jesus Christ. If this is not true, then there is no "new message" in Christian teaching and Jesus Christ is not a true Saviour.

So convinced am I now that this assurance of immediate felicity after death is the point of vital difference between true Christian teaching and everything that has gone before, that if it were not true I would renounce Christian teaching entirely. If Christ's work and teaching did not put an end to the necessity of further expiation for sin after death, then He would not have been the promised Saviour and the Christ of God. He would be an impostor.

Among the religions that teach reincarnation may be counted Roman Catholicism, since its teaching of purgatory means that an indefinite period of expiation and suffering in another world is necessary (with very few exceptions) before the disembodied spirits of men can be sufficiently purified to enter into eternal bliss. In order to explain how a spirit can suffer the pains of material fire in purgatory, the Roman theologians have invented a theory that it takes on another kind of body—the nature of which they do not define—in which the suffering is felt.

In modern America the Roman Catholic Church tries to hide from Protestants its real teaching that the souls in purgatory suffer from actual fire. But St. Thomas Aquinas teaches that the pains of purgatory are as violent as hell. Cardinal (now Saint) Bellarmine declares: *"It is the same sensible punishment which the sinner ought to have suffered in hell, with the exception of its eternity."* Pope Benedict XIV also confirms this in his book, "On the Sacrifice of the Mass." *Our Sunday Visitor*, popular Catholic weekly paper, in its issue of November 26, 1945, put it very luridly as follows: *"Purgatory is Real: a Suburb of Hell . . . the sense pains of Purgatory equal those of hell. Which means the temperature is about the same in both regions."*

The existence of purgatory is a dogma of Roman Catholic faith, binding under pain of damnation in hell, and everyone who denies it is "anathematized" (cursed) by the solemn decree of the Council of Trent (*Sess. XXII*, c. 2) as follows:

"If any one saith that after the gift of justification has been received, to every penitent sinner the guilt is remitted and the debt of eternal punishment is blotted out in such a way that no debt of temporal punishment remains to be discharged either in this world or in the next in Purgatory, before the entrance to the Kingdom of heaven can be opened to him: let him be anathema."

In other words, if you don't believe in purgatory you are sure to go to hell.

The doctrine of purgatory is based upon the Roman Catholic division of punishment for sin into *eternal* (in hell) and *temporal* (in purgatory), as well as its arbitrary division of sin into *mortal* and *venial*. It is scarcely necessary to prove how entirely contradictory the whole dogma of purgatory is of Scripture teaching, which assures us that: *"There is now no condemnation to them that are in Christ Jesus"* *(Rom.* 8:1), and that, *"Being justified by His blood, we are saved from wrath through Him"* (*Rom.* 5: 9). And again: *"God hath not appointed us unto wrath, but to obtain salvation by our Lord Jesus Christ, who died for us, that, whether we wake or sleep, we should live together with Him."* (*I Thess.* 5: 9,10).

Evangelical Protestant teaching repudiates the Council of Trent's dogma of purgatory and its accompanying anathemas by boldly declaring that the spirits of those who are justified by Christ's saving work enter *at once* into joy and felicity, to be consummated at the second coming of Christ. Even before the death of Christ, the souls of the just did not suffer torture in the temporary state which the New Testament calls *Hades* (*Acts* 2: 31). For these souls were in the happy portion of it called *paradise*. *"This day,"* Christ promised the penitent thief on the cross, *"thou shalt be with me in paradise."* (*Luke* 23: 43).

It should not be surprising that the greater part of the human race is content with this doctrine of other lives of purgation after death through their own suffering for sins committed in this life. *Belief in re-*

incarnation and purgatory has a certain human attractiveness. It gives the hope of another opportunity of earning salvation under different conditions. This is especially attractive to those who believe in the Roman Catholic doctrine of purgatory, since the danger of hell for ever is removed by confession to a priest after sinning and especially before they die. As long as assurance is given that eternal punishment in hell can be avoided, a 'devil-may-care' attitude can be taken toward the mere *temporal* punishment to be suffered in purgatory. For no matter how long or indefinite this may be, the Roman Catholic is promised heaven in the end if he conforms to the regulations and disciplines of the Church and accepts the ministrations of its priests.

Furthermore, the doctrine of reincarnation and purgatory is humanly attractive because *it affords a way of compensating for an easy, self-indulgent life.* This is evident to those who know the teachings and practices of Roman Catholicism. Men by nature will yield to excess of indulgence, even though they know of the penalty to be paid afterwards, as long as they are fairly sure that opportunity will be allowed to compensate for its evil after-effects. *Sin loses much of its fear if the sinner is told he can make compensation himself for it by penance in this life or by purgation in another life.*

There is therefore a practical policy behind the teaching of Roman Catholicism that man himself can atone for his sins even after he dies. It makes more work for the priests, and extends their importance as alleged saviours of the countless dead as well as of the

living. To take salvation out of the hands both of the
sinner himself and the priest, as Evangelical Christianity does, would not only leave no need for the
priest, but would also act as a deterrent to the sinner
himself. In this Evangelical teaching accountability
as well as suffering for sin are placed upon another—
Jesus Christ—who alone takes full responsibility and
alone can fully satisfy for sin. This true Christian
teaching appeals to the finer instincts of man which
make him hesitate to do something for which another,
not himself, will have to suffer.

*The real evil of the Roman Catholic doctrine of
purgatory is the dishonor it casts upon the redeeming
work of the Incarnate Son of God.* Excuse may be
made for the doctrine of reincarnation in religions
that do not profess to believe in Jesus Christ and his
saving work. These do not set themselves up as followers of a Christ who made perfect and complete atone-
ment for sin. *Purgatory as a Christian doctrine takes
away from the fullness of Christ's love for his Church,
and is a denial of the completeness and sufficiency of
his sacrifice and mediatorial work.*

Dr. H. W. Dearden in his splendid work, *Modern
Romanism Examined,* concludes his chapter on purgatory as follows:

"If redemption had been entrusted to an archangel, the possible need of supplementing his mediatorial work might have been tolerated. But when it
is 'God in Christ' who has taken our nature and laid
down his life for the specific purpose of 'reconciling
the world unto himself,' and who has made 'propitiation for the sins of the whole world' on the altar of the

cross, this constant attempt, or rather injunction, to supplement our Lord's work of expiation and redemption as if it were inherently deficient, is an act of disloyalty to our Lord himself, injurious to the Church which exalts itself instead of Christ, and a sore hindrance to the soul's present enjoyment of 'joy and peace in believing' (*Rom.* 15: 13)."

CHAPTER TEN

PAGAN ORIGINS OF PURGATORY

I HAVE DISCOVERED that in all pagan religions the doctrine of a purgatory after death and prayers for the dead have always held an important place. By this means a second chance was left open to sinners who were unrepentant and consciously unfit for heaven. For this purpose a 'middle state' was invented in which guilt could be removed in the future world by means of purgatorial pains.

In Greece the doctrine of a purgatory was taught by the very chief of the philosophers. Thus Plato,[1] speaking of the future judgment of the dead, holds out the hope of final deliverance for all, but maintains that, of "those who are judged," some must *first* "proceed to a subterranean place of judgment, where they shall *sustain the punishment they have deserved.*" In pagan Rome, purgatory was also held up before the minds of men. Virgil, celebrated poet of pagan Rome, describing its different tortures, puts it thus:

"Nor can the grovelling mind,
In the dark dungeon of the limbs confined,
Assert the native skies, or own its heavenly kind.
Nor death itself can wholly wash their stains;
But long-contacted filth, even in the soul, remains;
The relics of inveterate vice they wear,

---

[1] Plato, *Phaedrus*, p. 249, A, B.

And spots of sin obscene in every face appear.
For this are various penances enjoined;
And some are hung to bleach upon the wind,
Some plunged in water, others purged in fires,
Till all the dregs are drained, and all the rust expires.
All have their Manes, and those Manes bear.
The few so cleansed to these abodes repair,
And breathe in ample fields the soft Elysian air.
Then are they happy, when by length of time
The scurf is worn away of each committed crime,
No speck is left of their habitual stains,
But the pure ether of the soul remains." [2]

This pagan teaching that there is no power that
can so cleanse the soul that at death it can dare "assert
the native skies or own its heavenly kind," without
being purged in tormenting fire, is still officially proclaimed by the Roman Catholic Church today. *The
Cathedral Bulletin,* official monthly publication of St.
Patrick's Cathedral in New York, in its issue for
August, 1947, declares as follows: *"Thank God that
there is a purgatory here and hereafter, where our
poor, imperfect love is purged of its dross, made pure
and perfect; for then, and only then, can we stand
before Him unashamed and unafraid."* This publication bears the names of Cardinal Spellman, three other
bishops, three monsignori and six priests.

All of them are contradicted by the New Testament teaching which definitely asserts (*Heb.* 10: 19):
*"Having therefore, brethren, the boldness to enter into
the holiest by the blood of Jesus, by a new and living*

---
[2] Dryden's *Virgil.*

way . . ." Virgil the pagan poet can be excused for teaching the necessity of a purgatory after death, since he did not know Christ and had no New Testament to reveal to him the "new and living way" by which we can be completely cleansed and by which we can dare to "draw near to God with a true heart in full assurance of faith." No such excuse can be made for the cardinals, bishops, monsignori and priests of the Roman Catholic Church.

In Egypt, substantially the same doctrine of purgatory was taught. But once this doctrine of purgatory was admitted into the popular mind, then the door was opened to all manner of priestly extortions. Prayers for the dead go hand in hand with purgatory. No prayers can be completely efficacious without the priest as an intermediary and no priestly functions can be rendered unless there be *special pay* for them. Therefore, in every land we find the pagan priesthood "devouring widows' houses," and making merchandise of the tender feelings of sorrowing relatives sensitively alive to the immortal happiness of their beloved dead.

From all quarters there is the same testimony as to the burdensome character and the *expense* of these posthumous devotions. One of the oppressions under which people in Roman Catholic countries groan, is the periodical nature of special devotions, for which they are required to pay, when death has carried away a member of a Catholic family. Not only are there funeral services and funeral dues for the repose of the departed at the time of burial, but the priest pays repeated visits afterwards to the family for the same purpose, which entail heavy expense, beginning with what is called "the month's mind" mass, that is, a service in behalf of the deceased when a month after death has elapsed.

A similar practice was in vogue in ancient Greece: "*There the Argives sacrificed on the thirtieth day* (after death) *to Mercury as the conductor of the dead.*"[3] In India there are many burdensome services of the Sradd'ha, or funeral obsequies for the repose of the dead, and for securing the proper efficacy of these it is taught that "donations of cattle, land, gold, silver, and other things," should be made by the man himself at the approach of death, or, "if he be too weak, by another in his name."[4]

How perfectly identical this is with Roman Catholic teaching about purgatory today in America, may be seen from the following advertisement which appeared in *Our Sunday Visitor,* popular Catholic weekly newspaper to which I have already referred, in its issue of August 11, 1946:

"ARE YOU INSURED?"

"*Write and ask about our plan to offer the Gregorian Masses after your death. This is real insurance for your soul.*"

'Gregorian Masses' for a soul in purgatory are thirty in number and must be offered consecutively. Minimum price is $30.00. It is believed and taught that Christ appeared to St. Gregory and promised that He would release souls from purgatory on pay-

---

[3] Muller, *History of the Dorians,* vol. ii, p. 405.
[4] *Asiatic Reseaches,* vol. vii, pp. 239-40.

ment of the money—and even before the thirty masses are said.

In all pagan religions the case is the same. In
Tartary, "The Gurjumi, or prayers for the dead,"
says the *Asiatic Journal,* "are very expensive."[5] In
Greece, says Suidas, *"the greatest and most expensive
sacrifice was the mysterious sacrifice called the
Telete,"*[6] a sacrifice which, according to Plato, "was
offered for the living and the dead, and was supposed
to free them from all the evils to which the wicked are
liable when they have left this world."[7] In Egypt the
exactions of the priests for funeral dues and masses
for the dead were equally burdensome. "The priests,"
says Wilkinson, "induced the people to expend large
sums on the celebration of funeral rites; and *many
who had barely sufficient to obtain the necessaries of
life* were anxious to save something for the expenses
of their death. For, besides the embalming process,
which sometimes cost a talent of silver, about $1,000,
the tomb itself was purchased at an immense expense;
and numerous demands were made upon the estate of
the deceased for the celebration of prayer and other
services for the soul."

"The ceremonies," he tells us elsewhere, "consist-
ed of a sacrifice similar to those offered in the temples,
vowed for the deceased to one or more gods (as Osiris,
Anubis, and others connected with Amentin); incense
and libations were also presented; and a prayer was
sometimes read, the relations and friends being present as mourners. They even joined their prayers to
those of the priest. The priest who officiated at the

[5] *Asiatic Journal,* vol. xvii, p. 143.
[6] *Suidas,* vol. ii, p. 879 B.
[7] *Plato,* vol. ii, pp. 364-65.

burial service was selected from the grade of Pontiffs who wore the leopard skin; but various other rites were performed by one of the minor priests to the mummies, previous to their being lowered into the pit of the tomb after that ceremony. Indeed, they continued to be administered at intervals, as long as the family paid for their performance."[8]

Such was the operation of the doctrine of purgatory and prayers for the dead among avowed and acknowledged pagans, and it differs in no way from the operation of the same doctrine as taught by the Roman Catholic Church today. There are the same extortions in both. The Roman Catholic doctrine of purgatory is purely pagan, and cannot for a moment stand in the light of Scripture. For those who die in Christ no purgatory *is*, or *can* be needed; for *"the blood of Jesus Christ, God's Son, cleanseth from all sin."* If this be true, where can there be the need for any other cleansing? On the other hand, for those who die without personal union with Christ, and consequently unwashed, unjustified, unsaved, there can be no other cleansing; for, while *"he that hath the Son hath life, he that hath not the Son hath not life."*

Thus the whole doctrine of purgatory is a system of plain pagan imposture, dishonoring God, deluding men who live in sin with the hope of atoning for it after death, and cheating them at once out of their property and their salvation. In the pagan purgatory, fire, water, wind, were represented (as may be seen from the lines of Virgil) as combining to purge away the stain of sin. In the purgatory of the Roman Cath-

---

[8] *Wilkinson*, vol. ii, p. 94, vol. v, pp. 383-84.

olic Church, ever since the days of Pope Gregory, *fire* itself has been the grand means of purgation.[9]

Out of this labyrinth of pagan deceit, this maze of lies about the vital issue of life or death for my soul, I have been delivered. How blessed it is to know that the blood of the Lamb, applied as a free gift by the Spirit of God to the most defiled conscience, completely purges it from sin and dead works. Surely the gratitude of a converted priest should be even greater than that of the ordinary converted sinner, because of the assurance that we are saved, not by trusting in the 'sacrifice of the mass,' which can no more take away sin than the blood of bulls or goats, but by the one complete sacrifice of Calvary offered by God's eternal and well-beloved Son.

So deep is the deception in the Roman Catholic labyrinth, that men like Monsignor Fulton J. Sheen, reputed and honored as leading lights of spiritual wisdom for others, are completely lost in it. In his recent book, *Preface to Religion*,[10] Monsignor Sheen talks from one side of his mouth (in chapter 5) of being "re-made," "re-created," and "born again," and being "incorporated into the risen Christ," as if he were a teacher of Evangelical Christianity who believed in being saved "to the uttermost" by the finished sacrifice of Christ offered on Calvary once and forever. Farther on (in chapter 9) he speaks with the other side of his mouth on the necessity of purgatory, where all, even after priestly absolution, must expiate for their sins, *"confined to that prison of purifying fire."*

---

[9] *Catechismus Romanus*, pars. i, art. 5, sect. 5, p. 50.
[10] P. J. Kenedy and Sons, New York, 1946.

"These souls," he declares, "have not the strength to bind their own wounds, and heal their own scars: it remains for us who are still strong and healthy . . . to heal their wounds and make them whole that they might join the ranks of the victors and march in the procession of the conquerors."

The only logical answer I can find to account for such spiritual foolishness is that Monsignor Sheen is either hopelessly blinded by the devil's deceit, or is a conscious hyprocrite, knowingly speaking in contradictions so as to protect the power of his priesthood over the countless dead.

The thought of all this inspires me with a tender compassion for the deluded people of the Roman Catholic Church, of which I also was ordained a priest to teach the same delusions. Free now in the liberty wherewith Christ has made us free, I cannot but appeal to all true Christian people to see to it that neither we nor our children may ever again be entangled in that yoke of bondage.

(For a more extended analysis of the Roman Catholic doctrine of purgatory as compared with its counterpart in pre-Christian pagan religions, see Alexander Hislop's splendid treatise, *The Two Babylons*, chap. 5, sec. 3, which I have drawn upon for the quotations above.)

CHAPTER ELEVEN

KEYS FOR THE WRONG LOCK

KEYS are a symbol of power, the power to open up and distribute, or to lock up and deny things necessary or longed-for—be it jam in the cupboard, electric energy in the dynamo, or the power of God in the kingdom of heaven.

Everyone knows the "key story" which has been repeated throughout the centuries by the Church of Rome. It was told to me like a bed-time story when I was a child: How only to Peter the apostle did Jesus Christ give the keys of the kingdom of heaven with all power over men and nations. And how only to the popes of Rome as the rightful successors of Saint Peter can these keys be handed down for all time. This makes a pope in Rome, as the present Pope Pius XII reminded all Americans in a recent radio broadcast, *"the only one authorized to act and teach for God."*

Thus this same Eugenio Pacelli, under the name of Pope Pius XII, residing on Vatican Hill in Rome, would today be the only one who has in his pocket these keys that can open the flood-gates of the power of the spirit of God and heal the ills of the world. Hitler was tearing Christian civilization to shreds when Pope Pius XII made the above awesome announcement. This means that he could have stopped Hitler and the other war-guilty dictators and brought peace and salvation to all men. Instead, he helped their evil deeds. It was this same Eugenio Pacelli who helped Hitler to power by putting his signature to the Vatican's concordat with Nazi Germany in 1933.

This key story may sound all right when things are going well with the world. When they go wrong, however, and criminal men ride their apocalyptic horses of tyranny and brutality, death and destruction over the face of the earth, we may well ask why the power of God is kept locked up by the one man who boasts of having the keys to release it. Today more than ever before, with the threat of atomic destruction hanging over the whole world, this power of God is the only effective weapon to save us all from complete annihilation. If Eugenio Pacelli has any keys at all, he must either refuse to put them to their proper use, or else they must fit the wrong set of locks.

Jesus Christ plainly warned against those who falsely profess to have the sole power to open up or lock the gates of heaven. In dire condemnation of them he says: *"Ye shut up the kingdom of heaven against men: for ye neither go in yourselves, neither suffer ye them that are entering to go in."* (*Matt.* 23:13).

The strangest paradox of Roman Catholic teaching is its claim, on the one hand, that Saint Peter was the first pope and Bishop of Rome; and its refusal, on the other hand, to listen to and obey the teaching of Saint Peter as written down in the New Testament. If a pope's words are accepted as infallible today, one would think that Roman Catholics, including the pope himself, would accept as even more infallible what Peter decreed in New Testament teaching. They should at least accept with equal authority Peter's writings and the encyclical letters and decrees of the popes of Rome down the centuries. The reason why Peter's instructions are hushed up happens to be because what he decreed is a condemnation of the very position of the pope and his Roman *curia*.

Saint Peter wrote two epistles or letters, and in the first he solemnly instructs his co-workers in the Christian ministry how the Christian Church should be governed. In chapter 5, verses 1 to 3, he decrees as follows:

"The elders which are among you I exhort, who am also an elder, and a witness of the sufferings of Christ, and also a partaker of the glory that shall be revealed:

"Feed the flock of God which is among you, taking the oversight thereof, not by constraint, but willingly; not for filthy lucre, but of a ready mind;

"Neither being as lords over God's heritage, but being examples to the flock."

Here we have Peter, speaking with authority as Christ's co-worker and chief of the apostles, making it clear that the set-up of Christ's Church must be first of all *democratic*, not authoritarian. He calls himself an "elder" (*presbyter*, which has nothing at all to do with a sacrificing priest), equal to the other apostles and Christian leaders whom he also calls elders. He exhorts them to minister to the faithful, not by forceful methods but in a way that will bring free response.

Most important of all, he forbids the Church leaders to become "lords" over the people. The full significance of this can only be understood from the

Greek word which Peter used for "lords." That word in the Greek is *katakuriontes,* which the Latin Vulgate version of the New Testament translates as *dominantes.* But if Peter's own Greek word *katakuriontes* is closely examined, it will be found to contain the word *curia,* which was the autocratic governing body of the Roman Empire of the Caesars. To Peter himself and to those he addressed in his letter, the full significance of this word was very plain. For the Roman *curia* at that time ruled the world with an iron fist. It was as plain to people in his time as if he told the leaders of the Christian Church today: *"Don't be Fascists or Nazis!"*

In other words, Peter plainly decreed that the method of governing the Christian Church must not be patterned after that of Caesar—or sawdust imitators of him in the twentieth century. He wants it to be the very opposite of the curial system of Rome. It was to be a democratic system, with no one lording it over the others, and the people corresponding freely, not by coercion.

It is scarcely necessary for me to mention the fact that the Roman Catholic Church acts directly opposite to these instructions of Saint Peter, its so-called first pope. After the fourth century, the Bishops of Rome stepped right into Caesar's shoes, took on his pagan title of Pontifex Maximus, the Supreme High Priest of the Roman religion, sat down on Caesar's throne and wrapped themselves in Caesar's gaudy trappings. Everything about the pope and his court today is as it was at the court of the Caesars in ancient Rome. Through the very Roman *curia* which

Peter abhorred and condemmed, the Vatican has ruled the Catholic Church to this day.

Not content with claiming the autocratic power of the Caesars in religion and politics, the popes of Rome also claimed to have the power of Almighty God himself. By infallible decree the pope has been made the very mouthpiece of God on earth, God's sole deputy. He can impose dogmatic decrees under pain of excommunication and death in this life, and the loss of eternal salvation in the next. Absolute power corrupts absolutely.

On these sky-high claims rests the whole foundation of the Church of Rome. But no pope will ever mention that they are in direct contradiction of the instructions that Saint Peter set down in the very book of the Gospels.

On other points too, the Church of Rome has completely perverted the word of the Gospel. Jesus Christ (*Matt.* 23 : 7) distinctly says: *"Call no man your father on the earth, for one is your father which is in heaven."* Christ here meant spiritual father, one who usurps the place of our Father in heaven. But not only does the very name pope (*papa*) mean father as designating the pope's spiritual office, but every Roman Catholic priest has to be called "Father" by the people. Another title of the pope is *Sua Santità di Nostro Signore,* "The Holiness of Our Lord." Christ taught his apostles and disciples to be poor and humble, not lavishly rich and authoritative. Yet the pope of Rome, with his *curia* of cardinals and bishops, dresses in the most sumptuous and expensive garments of cloth of gold and lace studded with precious gems.   In Febru-

ary, 1946, when thirty-two new cardinals were created by Pope Pius XII, Americans were shocked to
learn that the scarlet robes alone of every new cardinal's outfit cost $10,000. Everything the pope touches
—even his telephone and microphone—is of gold.

In view of all this, how can the pope, cardinals
and bishops be, as Saint Peter exhorts, "examples"
to the people? And how can the people, in turn, imi-
tate them, since their lives are so different from those
of the people to whom they are supposed to minister?
Far from carrying out Saint Peter's instructions not
to be "lords" over the people and not to coerce them,
the leaders of the Church of Rome have always resisted democratic principles of equality and brotherhood and allied themselves to despotic kings and authoritarian governments. In our own time, the Roman
curia at the Vatican bound itself by solemn concor-
dats and alliances to the Nazi-fascist dictatorships
of Mussolini, Hitler, Franco and others.

To me, who once served the altars of the Church
of Rome, it becomes more sadly apparent, the farther
I draw away from it, how much it has perverted both
the form and teaching of the true Church of Christ.
My work and prayers now are directed to the end
that, by the preservation of our democratic freedoms,
the Catholic people in America will some day discover
the truth and, instead of blindly submitting to the
curial dictatorship of the Vatican, accept the democratic, Gospel teaching of Saint Peter.

The growth of this ecclesiastical dictatorship of
the Roman papacy began with the need for a 'president' who was later designated as 'bishop' or overseer

over the other elders. This led to distinctions between
ranks and authority, and, step by step, to a plan of
Church government patterned after the law and regulation of Roman military regimentation, that was
not sanctioned by the New Testament. The bishop
soon extended his rule over several congregations
called a 'diocese,' and thus established one-man rule
over a district of Churches. Later, many dioceses were
grouped together under one head called a 'metropoli-
tan,' similar to the archbishop of today.

These departures from New Testament Church
government continued until there developed a trend
toward religious imperialism in the Christian Church.
The last stage in its development was the establishment of the Roman papacy with its *curia* and hierarchy, at the apex of which was the Bishop of Rome as
pope and autocratic monarch. This was in the year
606, when the title of "Universal Bishop of the
Church" was bestowed upon him. But the papacy did
not reach the zenith of its power until the time of
Pope Gregory VII, in the year 1073.

Consummation of this growth of universal power
of the Bishop of Rome took place in 1870, when Pope
Pius IX, by the dogmatic decree of papal infallibility,
proclaimed himself and all popes to come after him
absolute dictator of the entire Christian Church. Were
he to visit Rome today, Peter, the gentle elder of the
New Testament Church, would be horrified to find
himself and Jesus Christ impersonated by the be-
jewelled occupant of the throne of Caesar on Vatican
Hill. For Peter was taught by Christ not to rule over
the people the same as "the princes of the Gentiles

exercise dominion over them." He heard from his Master's own lips the command: *"But it shall not be so among you: but whosoever will be great among you, let him be your minister: And whosoever will be chief among you, let him be your servant."* (*Matt.* 20: 25-27).

These departures from the spirit and teaching of the New Testament Church, and from the instructions laid down by Saint Peter himself, were the natural consequences of the self-interest and ambition of men to gain supreme and unlimited power over other men. They led, as history bears witness, to the spirit of tyranny which destroyed the congregational or democratic form of Church government in Europe. For ecclesiastical power succeeds where other institutions fail in forcing masses of trusting people to give up their liberty. Designing politicians, themselves scheming at all times to lord it over their fellow men, have always been quick to align themselves with those in supreme positions of power in the religious world.

It was thus in Jerusalem when the priests of the Jewish religion conspired with the Roman politicians to crucify Christ because they feared the moral reform his teaching threatened to bring about. And it is thus today in the big cities of the United States where the priests, the police and the politicians combine to control politics and the press. The Roman Catholic cardinal's chancery office in New York City is known to all as the political "power house."

But the politicians in the end become mere tools of the Church authorities. They are forced to serve as partners of the more dominant church power for fear of losing their own positions if they should act against the wishes of their ecclesiastical overlords. Europe has been bedevilled for fifteen centuries with this unbeatable combination of political-ecclesiastical control.   Protestant America is now faced with its appearance on this side of the Atlantic.   In the struggle to overcome it, the only effective remedy is a return to the spirit and pure teaching of the Gospel of Christ.

CHAPTER TWELVE

HOW WE ARE SANCTIFIED

SANCTIFICATION, in the true Christian sense, means a *setting apart,* or a *separation to,* and indicates a new place occupied. The sinner is separated by the Spirit of God to the working of holiness by the divine law of growth, not by human merit. It has nothing to do with feelings or experiences, but is a conformity of the will to God's will by His spirit. *"This is the will of God, even your sanctification"* (1 *Thess.* 4: 3).

NOT A 'LAUNDERING' PROCESS

In Roman Catholic teaching, sanctification, like everything else in its theology, is an *external process* dependent upon the works of the sinner using the seven sacraments of the Church as his only means of obtaining grace. These seven sacraments are pictured as seven channels of grace in which the sinner must wash his soul from sin, so that when he dirties it again, he has to return for another washing.

Nothing could be farther from the truth of Christian teaching than this crude "laundering process" that is taught to the Catholic people as the only way in which they can become holy. It is poles apart from what is taught in the Scriptures which make it clear, before everything else, that holiness is the entering into a new life by an *act of God*, which is good forever. The Prophet Jeremiah tells us that not even a cleanser as strong as *potassium nitrate* can wash a soul from sin: *"For though thou wash thee with nitre, and take thee much soap, yet thine iniquity is marked before me saith the Lord God"* (*Jer.* 2: 22).

Sanctification is not a mere imitation of Christ, but an identification with Him, and, as a consequence, an assimilation to Him. It is a *relationship* rather than a *quality*, a *condition*, not a *characteristic*, a *union*, not an *attribute*. *"Your life is hid with Christ in God"* (*Col.* 3: 3). *"We are in Him that is true"* (1 *John* 5: 20); *"He that sanctifieth and they that are sanctified are all of one"* (*Heb.* 2: 11).

Rev. Linus Riordan, a Roman priest, in a series of articles on holiness in the Catholic *Register* in November, 1946, defines holiness as "nearness to God," which is attained only *"in direct proportion to the manner in which they* [Catholics] *follow the Church's dogmas and counsels; obey her commandments, attend Mass, and receive the sacraments."* Continuing, he describes holiness as a "ray" from the Church: "To draw men more quickly to that Church, He willed that there should shine forth from His Church a ray so brilliant that if men follow the path that it lights they will find the source of salvation, the true Church. *That ray is holiness."*

The glaring illogicality of this teaching of the Catholic Church concerning salvation, sanctification and forgiveness of sins, can easily be seen from the fundamental fact of the Scripture teaching that, in the first place, *man must have life before he can act at all in a spiritual way.* "*We thus judge,*" says Paul, in strict logic, "*that if one died for all, then were all dead*" (*2 Cor.* 5: 14). Sanctification is a function of a *live* man, not something that is applied to one spiritually *dead,* and which leaves him still dead after its application. All humanity and its acts are nothing but vanity before God and without any value whatsoever in His sight except it be created anew in Christ Jesus: "*As many as received him, to them gave He the power to become the sons of God . . .*" (*John* 1: 12).

Adam is dead. God's standard of holiness has slain him and all his children. The most beautiful *natural* life ever lived cannot begin to measure up to the holy requirements of God. Adam and his sons cannot be renewed, patched up, or made over by any human means—even by a Church with seven sacraments and its claim to exclusive existence by divine right.

As in other matters, Catholic Church teaching about sanctification throws us off balance by confusing that which is of the earth, earthy, with what should be the new man in Christ. It confuses the earthen vessel with the treasure that should be in it. The earthen vessel—"the image of the earthy"—is *never* sanctified; the treasure within is *forever* sanctified. In other words, we are not sanctified as *sons of Adam,* but as "*sons of God.*" On the earth side, we are told: "*If we say that we have no sin, we deceive ourselves, and the truth is not in us*" (1 *John* 1: 8). On the spiritual side we can exult in the fact that: "*We know that whosoever is born of God sinneth not*" (1 *John* 5: 18).

SANCTIFICATION AS 'ABSOLUTE POSITION'

As an act of God, sanctification is a *fixed condition* of the creature that is assimilated to Christ. *"Justification is organically connected with sanctification; grace the supreme motive of obedience,"* says Bishop H. C. G. Moule in his commentary on the book of Romans in the *Cambridge Bible for Schools and Colleges.* Man, by nature guilty and defiled, is by the one and the same act both justified and sanctified. By virtue of the blood of Christ, God has declared men righteous and called men holy. Faith in Christ places us forever among the saints—*"Among them which are sanctified by faith that is in me"* (*Acts* 26:18). The justified man is a sanctified man. *"Those whom he predestined, them he has also called; and those whom he has called, them he has also justified, and those whom he justified, them he has also glorified"* (*Rom.* 8: 30).

Thus justification and sanctification go hand in hand with forgiveness which, for this reason, is not, as in Roman Catholic teaching, a periodical laundering of the soul by the absolution of a priest in confession, but the gift of a whole new soul won by the offering of Christ. Since that offering of Christ is perfect and final, the forgiven sinner is made perfect in holiness before God. *The forgiven man is a sanctified man.*

Sir Robert Anderson, in his valuable work, *The Gospel and Its Ministry,* puts it this way:

"Perfection is the only standard that can avail with God; and full provision has been made, not only to make us, but to keep us, perfect.

"We stand at an immeasurable distance from all the low thoughts of God, and light views of sin, that alone can lend an air of plausibility to such a delusion that any cultivation of piety, or attainment in sanctity, can ever give us the right to seek His presence, or fitness to be there. It is only and altogether in virtue of the blood of Christ that the saintliest saint on earth can hold fellowship with God. A higher title is impossible, and no lower will avail.

"No change of scene can add virtue to the blood of Christ, therefore heaven itself can add nothing to the holiness in which we stand by reason of that blood. No holy living upon earth can add to the intrinsic perfectness of Christ Himself."

The individual thus forgiven and sanctified is the passive recipient of a work performed—not by any pope, bishop, priest or Church—but by Him who alone can free us from the law of sin and death. *"But of him are ye in Christ Jesus, who of God is made unto us wisdom, and righteousness, and sanctification and redemption"* (1 Cor. 1: 30).

SANCTIFICATION AS A 'WALK'

As forgiven, justified and sanctified forever, the believer is then, and then only, in a position to be governed by divine motives, applied by grace, to yield his members unto holiness. This new position entails new obligations: *"The Love of Christ constraineth us"* —that henceforth we should not live unto ourselves but unto Him (2 Cor. 5: 14-15). There is no stronger motivating force than the love of God. Having been absolutely sanctified, the Christian will continue in holiness, as he continues to grow in grace. He is a new creature in Christ, a partaker of the divine nature, and thus can walk the path of holiness. This *practical* aspect of holiness is the logical sequence of the *fixed* or *positional* aspect of it. If we are fixed in this new position, we shall have a "new walk."

Just as works are the *effect*, not the *cause* of salvation, so sanctification will produce a holy walk, not a holy walk produce sanctification, as Roman Catholic teaching insists. Sanctification makes us citizens of heaven, but we haven't yet reached home. As a result, the walk may become defiled. In *Ephesians* 5, Paul explains how we must walk as "followers of God." Only the saints, blessed with all spiritual blessings in Christ, could be so exhorted. God never exhorts the unbeliever to holiness. Only the man in Christ can have "understanding what the will of the Lord is."

In his effort to explain this true Christian aspect of sanctification Saint Augustine bubbled over into his seemingly paradoxical aphorism: *"Ama Deum et fac quod vis"*—"Love God and do as you like." Both Saint Augustine and Martin Luther held that a Christian is so sanctified in the absolute sense, by God's act, that irrespective of his natural tendencies, he cannot but live and act "as becometh holy persons." *"He that saith he abideth in him ought himself also to walk even as He walked"* (1 *John* 2: 6). For this "walking even as He walked" is not a straining after perfection in the flesh, but the working *through us* of God's work *in us*. Luther saw so clearly the uselessness of the Catholic medieval teaching about sanctification and of the straining after the flesh and being

made "holy" by the "sacrifice of the Mass," and by
partaking of the seven sacraments, that he cried out:

*"Man's folly, however, is so prodigious that, in-
stead of embracing the message of grace with its
guarantee of the forgiveness of sin for Christ's sake,
man finds himself more laws to satisfy his conscience.
'If I live,' says he, 'I'll mend my life. I will do this, I
will do that.' Man, if you don't do the very opposite,
if you don't send Moses with the Law back to Mount
Sinai and take the hand of Christ, pierced for your
sins, you will never be saved.*

*"When the Law drives you to the point of
despair, let it drive you a little farther, let it drive you
straight into the arms of Jesus who says: 'Come unto
me, all ye that labor and are heavy laden, and I will
give you rest.' "* (Commentary on *Galatians*).

Paul put it more clearly still (*Phil.* 2: 13): *"For
it is God that worketh in you both to will and to do of
His good pleasure."*

In *Cambridge Bible Notes*, page 93 of the commentary on 1 *Thessalonians* by Geo. G. Findlay, we
read:

"God's will and our consecration to Him are the
double reason for leading a chaste life; and these two
reasons are one, the latter springing out of the former.

"Holy is the single word which by itself denotes
the Divine Character, as it is revealed to us in its
moral transcendence, in the awfulness and glory of
its absolute perfection, raised infinitely above all that
is earthly and sinful. Now it is the character of God
that constitutes His right to the consecration of those
to whom He is revealed. Our sanctification is the

acknowledgment of God's claim upon us as the Holy
One Who made us. This involves our assimilation to
His nature. In Him, first the character, then the
claim; in us, first the claim admitted, then the character impressed."

It can easily be seen that this true teaching of
Christian sanctification can have no place in Roman
Catholic theology. For it would switch sinners from
dependence on the Church, with its dogmas, counsels
and commandments, as Father Riordan, above quoted,
requires to complete and constant yielding to God
through Christ.

This would soon deprive the Church, as a system
of power, of its profitable control over its millions of
lost souls.

OUR COOPERATION

As a former priest of that Church converted, as
Paul was, to the ministry of God's Word and Truth
in all its fullness, I cannot too strongly emphasize that
the work of our salvation and sanctification is the
Lord's, both *positionally* and *continually*. From God's
point of view our sanctification is an *absolute act*,
fixed once and forever. From our *relative* point of
view it is a continuous process requiring our cooperation with that act and will of God. *"He acts that we
may act,"* Saint Augustine says (*De gratia et lib.
arbitrio*, ch. 16, p. 32), *"by giving to our will all the
necessary strength."*

We are not relieved, therefore, of the responsibility of cooperating with this grace, both to will and to
love to do that which we know we ought to do for our

own salvation, and also to cooperate with God's will for the salvation of others. There is only an apparent contradiction between God's will and our cooperation. This is due to the fact that what appears to us kaleidoscopically broken up into millions of fragments of human time, is one complete act in God's view of the eternal *now*.

CHAPTER THIRTEEN

JEZEBEL ABROAD IN AMERICA

NO ONE can fail to notice how much idolatry is flaunted in the faces of Christians today. Pictures of people suppliant before images abound in the secular press, and on tens of thousands of movie screens idolatrous displays and worshipping before images have become the regular diet of the American public. Protestants have become so accustomed to these things that they are beginning to lose the sense of shock to their Christian sensibilities. Our American cities, like Athens as Saint Paul saw it, are given over to idolatry, and the revived cult of Jezebel, both crude and cultured, finds an eager following.

Paganization of the life of a people is a gradual process. Satan does not make his initial attack in the open. He uses the 'softening up' process first, by introducing a disintegrating element, the evil of which, however, is hidden under a feeling of security and special privilege. He seduces the people of God with the attractive leaven of idolatry and its fond deceptions. He uses the evil and artful promoter of idolatrous teaching who has always been symbolized by the woman Jezebel.

The historic Jezebel was the idolatrous queen of the weak and wicked Ahab. She brought into Israel all the abominations of her heathen land. Cruel,

boasting and scheming, she boldly seized the God-
given inheritance of Naboth after causing his death.
She feasted at her table the infamous prophets of
Baal, and by cunning and cruelty silenced the true
prophets and worshippers of the Lord. So successful
was she in this, that Elijah thought he was the only
worshipper of the true God left in Israel.

This seducing Jezebel has been brought into our
midst in America. The abominations she has carried
with her from her heathen land have permeated all
the institutions of American life. They are to be seen
on the higher levels of art and literature as well as on
the low levels of base pleasure and amusement. Everything is, as it were, encrusted with it. In religion,
where she ranks as a prophetess, Jezebel sets forth
her fascinating deceptions—a monstrous mingling of
pagan and Christian elements, thus corrupting sound
doctrine and perverting the truth. In the Roman
Catholic Church she holds an exalted place and her
teaching is authoritative. There she is adept at dis-
guising her pagan ancestry under a thin veneer of
Christian phraseology.

Converts to Roman Catholicism like Mrs. Clare
Luce, prompted by Monsignor Fulton J. Sheen and
other priest-tutors, put forth specious arguments in
an effort to prove that Roman Catholics are not taught
to worship or pray *to* statues and images; that they
only pray *before* them and *to* the saints thus worshipped. Despite such plausible excuses, it cannot be
denied that Roman Catholicism has made the second
commandment of God of no effect among its people,
and teaches for Christian doctrine the precepts of its

Church, which are the commandments of men. In fact, it has entirely eliminated the wording of the second commandment from its version of the Decalogue in its catechisms and textbooks.[1]

On Mt. Sinai God, through Moses, spoke saying: *"Thou shalt not make unto thee any graven image or any likeness of anything that is in heaven above, or that is in the earth beneath, or that is in the water under the earth; Thou shalt not bow down thyself to them nor serve them."*

In order to explain the absence of the above commandment in Roman Catholic listings of the Decalogue, Catholic apologists will tell you, of course, that it is implicitly contained in the first commandment. But no matter what specious reasons they concoct, they cannot deny that they teach their people to make graven images and to bow down before them. This is a direct violation of the second commandment of God which specifically says: "Thou shalt *not* make unto thyself any graven image . . . Thou shalt *not* bow down thyself to them . . ." Roman Catholics do both. They not only make the images, but also bow down on bended knees before them, light candles to them and burn incense before them.

As a student and a priest in Rome, I had to officiate on Christmas night at the ceremony of carrying in procession a gorgeously dressed doll-image (*bambino*) of the infant Jesus under a Japanese umbrella.

---

[1] See, for example, *My Sunday Missal*, by Father Joseph Stedman, p. 299, and the versions of the Catholic *Baltimore Catechism*, taught in all parochial schools.

The image was placed on the high altar, hymns were sung to it and a priest, on bended knees, offered up incense before it. Then the little doll was presented to the congregation and each one kneeling kissed its stomach, inside of which we believed was a piece of the manger in which Christ was born. When we visited St. Peter's Basilica we were told that an indulgence could be gained by kissing the foot of a huge metal statue, supposed to be that of Saint Peter, but said to be actually an ancient image of Marcus Aurelius. All semblance of a foot had long disappeared, since it had been kissed away until only a smooth, polished piece of shapeless metal remained. Reporting the ceremonies in Ottawa, Canada, at the Marian Congress in June, 1947, *Life* magazine drew attention to the fact that a long procession of devout people knelt and kissed the foot of the giant statue of Mary "until the paint wore off its toes."

Pictures in an illustrated Italian newspaper of recent date [2] show that devout Catholic people in Naples still crawl prostrate on their stomachs before the images of their Madonnas and lick the ground with their tongues on their way to the statues. The New York Department of Health was obliged some years ago to put a stop to this practice among Italian people in the Bronx, because so many cases of tetanus resulted from it.

Down in their hearts, these Roman Catholic apologists know well enough that to bow down to an image is to confess worship to it. To all outward

[2] *L'Europeo,* April 5, 1947.

appearance and intent, this Roman Catholic practice of kneeling and bowing before images, lighting candles before them and offering up incense to them, differs in no way from the same practice of the Buddhists in India and of pagan people in other lands.

It is easy enough to understand how such corruption of religion begins and develops, and how God's awful prohibition and condemnation are eventually sidestepped. The natural heart of man is prone to the worship of images, is attracted to the tangible creature that in the end completely takes the place of God. This tendency springs from an aversion in the unregenerate heart to the perfect purity of God, despite a sense of dependence and guilt before God. The nearer man gets to the Holy One, the deeper becomes his sense of guilt. He naturally turns aside from a direct fellowship with One so much higher and holier than himself. He wants to be cleansed, but is unwilling either to confess himself a sinner, or to believe that God has so loved him that He gave His only-begotten Son as an all-sufficient Saviour from sin. He turns instead to what the apostle Paul calls the "beggarly elements" (*Gal.* 4: 9) and offers worship to an inferior creature, superior, however, to himself, in order to intercede for him. He feels that he can fellowship with this creature, who is inferior to God but much higher than himself, but still a creature on the same level with himself.

In this way all idolatry and paganization of religion are explained. And of this the Roman Catholic Church has taken profitable advantage. Its apologists make excuses for the worship of images and the use of inferior mediators by teaching that sinful man is not worthy to approach directly to God. Jesus Christ, they say, only brought justice, not mercy on earth, and that we must look to His mother and His special friends, the saints, to obtain mercy for us. Thus Mary is made the "Mediatrix of all graces," and they quote Saint Jerome that "God will not save us without the intercession of Mary."

Monsignor Fulton J. Sheen, in his recent book, *Preface to Religion,*[3] makes the same excuse to uphold the doctrine of purgatory. "The necessity of purgatory," he says, (p. 138), "is grounded upon the absolute purity of God. . . . If there were no purgatory, then the justice of God would be too terrible for words, *for who are they who would dare assert themselves pure enough and spotless enough to stand before the Immaculate Lamb of God?*"

Here can be seen Satan's deceptive teaching that no one can dare expect such mercy from God that all his sins can be completely forgiven, or that he can be saved "to the uttermost." This is true, of course, according to the teaching of the Roman Catholic Church that man can and must earn his own salvation. If by our own works we are saved, then indeed would we have to tremble and fear that we could never adequately atone for our sins. Then indeed would it be presumptuous to dare assert ourselves, as Monsignor Sheen says, pure enough and spotless enough to stand before the Immaculate Lamb of God! Then indeed would we have to seek and look to creatures higher

---

[3] P. J. Kenedy and Sons, 1946.

than us in sanctity who have earned more than we can, and to whom we could turn to intercede for us.

But that is the pagan way, the way of Jezebel. The true Christian way is, as Paul tells us (*Rom.* 5: 1, 2): *"Therefore being justified by faith, we have peace with God through our Lord Jesus Christ: By whom also we have access by faith into this grace wherein we stand, and rejoice in hope of the glory of God."* And again Paul flatly contradicts Monsignor Sheen (*Heb.* 10: 19-20): *"Having therefore, brethren, boldness to enter into the holiest by the blood of Jesus, by a new and living way, which He hath consecrated for us, through the veil, that is to say, His flesh."*

The Scripture teaching here clearly answers Monsignor Sheen's question and assures us that we *can* dare to enter into the holiest of holies, because of this "new and living way" of Christian teaching. Monsignor Sheen prefers the old pagan way, and he is logical and correct in saying that, by this pagan way of the unregenerate human heart, we can never be pure and spotless enough to stand before the terrifying presence of the Immaculate Lamb of God. But he surely is not so blind that he does not see the vast difference between the two. Complete spiritual blindness alone can excuse his failure to see it. If he is not spiritually blind, then he must be downright dishonest. He stands convicted of either one or the other by the above text of *Hebrews*.

I consider it a most extraordinary thing now that these defenders of saints and their images should seize upon the "absolute purity of God" as excuse for focusing the worship of their people downward to things of earth. By doing so, they are actually playing upon the aversion in the unregenerate heart of man to this perfect purity of God. They pander to the tendency in sinful man to spurn and reject the love of God as manifested in Christ, the one mediator and all-sufficient Saviour. This also serves to enhance and protect the power of the priest. It makes it necessary to set up an image which the people can see and which the priest can handle. For vain man must be master of his God. Priests in all religions have made it a cardinal principle of their teaching to make sure that the power of God they worship does not get out of their control. For this reason they made victims of their Gods so that they could handle and sacrifice them at will.

To be pitied therefore are the faithful followers of the priests of the Roman Catholic Church who are taught to reject the love of God and his plan of Christian redemption whereby they can be so purified by "a new and living way" that they can stand before God holy and blameless. Instead they are provided with idols and told that they dare not hope to have the boldness to enter into the holiest and have peace with God through our Lord Jesus Christ. They are not taught that our Lord has consecrated that new way for them through the shedding of his blood in his all-sufficient sacrifice on Calvary. Instead of that one great sacrifice of Calvary, they are given the idolatrous sacrifice of the mass, an affair of the hands and the magic of the breath of a priest whereby a sinful creature is believed to be able to create the God who made him!

Thus the wafer of bread in the Roman Catholic mass, made by human hands as all bread is made, is called God and adored on bended knees. This is the climax of the abominations of Jezebel. Without this caricature of Calvary, the Roman Catholic Church could not survive. *"Jezebel . . . painted her face and tired her head, and looked out at a window."* (II *Kings* 9: 30).

Today this same Jezebel has taken her place at the window. She is in the public eye. She is bold, for her time is short. She has painted her face, thus masking all the coarseness and vileness of her withered soul. She is defiant. She has decked her head, given herself a magnificent triple crown. Arrayed in her own pagan splendor she stands in the way of those who have a right to the crown of life and to receive the crown of glory. Jezebel derides the people of God —and Elijah has fled. He who stood on Mount Carmel and exposed the prophets of Baal for the miserable impostors they were and brought down the fierce judgment of God upon them, has quailed and fled before the threat of Jezebel. There is here, I think, a lesson for the timid Protestant leaders of our day, a picture of the people of God standing in awe in the face of onrushing idolatry, with few dissenting voices, all afraid of Jezebel!

But now that she flaunts her painted face from her lofty eminence, Jezebel's destruction, as of old, will be certain and swift. The fury of God will come up in his face and he will cast her down. For Christ, the image of the invisible God—the only image and only rightful object of worship—must conquer in the end. Jezebel, the idolatrous teacher of vanities and deceptions, will in due time be cast down and utterly consumed. Like the historical Jezebel who was eaten of dogs, all idolatrous systems of worship shall be found no more—*"so that they shall not say, This is Jezebel."*

CHAPTER FOURTEEN

PRIESTS AND EX-PRIESTS

THERE ARE OVER 40,000 Roman Catholic priests in the United States, a strange and somewhat mysterious body of men set apart by strict rule from other men like a caste of untouchables. They are very much of an enigma even to their own congregations. A small proportion of them—about 9,000—belong to the various religious orders of Jesuits, Benedictines, Franciscans, Dominicans and others. These are more rigorously cut off from the life of ordinary men than the 31,000 others called 'secular' priests who administer to the people in parishes, and who are expected to live *in* the world but to be not *of* it.

On the street these priests are distinguished from other men only by two inches of white collar turned back to front. But by their faithful congregations they are looked upon as superior beings who, by special divine dispensation, are placed high above them on richly decorated altars and dressed in cloth-of-gold and fine laces surrounded by burning tapers and sweet-smelling incense. Although they are honored in this way as superior to other men, these priests suffer great loneliness. For they are always conscious that they do not really differ from other men, and are stamped with a spiritual character that is more a fiction of popular sentiment than of special merit or calling.

Stranger still and more mysterious are those others, the so-called ex-priests of the Roman Catholic Church, who for conscience sake have abandoned the Roman priesthood. They are more numerous than is believed or allowed to be known. By forsaking the ranks of the priesthood they make themselves doubly apart from the world. For having done so, they are repudiated, completely misunderstood, even vilified by their families and former friends. They are truly outcasts from society. A sympathetic writer has coined a more charitable word for them—'Lost Shepherds.' These men first sacrificed their youth to a grandiose Church organization in what later proved to be a fruitless and deceptive ideal. Then they make themselves doubly martyrs by cutting themselves adrift, by way of protest, from their sole means of support and a reputable and highly honored position, suffering themselves to be branded as bad even in the eyes of their loved ones. Although Protestants owe the heritage of their faith to a similar protest by priests of the Roman Catholic Church in the sixteenth century, they are deceived today by false Roman Catholic propaganda into looking with suspicion upon all ex-priests.

Ex-priests are to be found where priests in good standing seldom appear: in the crush of subway trains and busses, in factories and work shops or at a clerk's desk in some city office. They are equal, if not superior in many instances, to most priests in high offices in the Church. One may wonder why such a great change should take place in a man's life by exchanging two inches of Roman collar for a regular collar and tie.

During the past ten years as director of Christ's Mission, I have known, contacted and worked with about a hundred ex-priests, including two former Roman Catholic bishops and several former Monsignori who held high positions in the Church of Rome. Not all of them have been converted to Evangelical Christianity; a goodly number of them, in fact, have remained agnostic and want to have nothing more to do with religion. This reaction to agnosticism and religious indifferentism is usual at first in almost all priests who come to a decision to abandon the priesthood after it fails them. This should not be held against them. It is proof rather that their ideals were of the highest order in the beginning. They then were taught to identify the Roman Catholic Church and its teachings with God and Christ. When the Church fails them, they naturally tend to think that God has failed them also.

Those who overcome this, and eventually arrive at spiritual peace and full assurance of salvation through the acceptance of Jesus Christ as full and perfect Saviour, have often a long, arduous road to travel. But as they emerge from the dark labyrinth of doubt and despair, they are amply compensated by the peace and joy, the assurance and light of the new and living way upon which they enter. The Divine Artist indeed chars well the sticks with which he traces His mysterious design. The soul of a priest is thus fashioned anew by traveling the royal road of the Cross.

Despite the general belief among Catholic people, ex-priests do not as a rule come from the 'bad priests' in the Church. Evil-living priests, in fact, do not voluntarily quit the ranks of the clergy, where economic security and a safe cloak for sex irregularities can easily be had. Most ex-priests I have known were most zealous as students for the priesthood and retained their pitch of spiritual fervor after ordination longer than others. I would say that the very fact that they had the courage to leave the priesthood is proof that their spiritual zeal was greater than those they left behind. For only a high pitch of spiritual enthusiasm, later thwarted by disillusionment, could produce enough courage to preserve self-integrity by sacrificing everything that seemed good in life a second time. Many have bravely faced this sacrifice in the almost hopeless hope that in this way, at least a part of their former high ideals might be salvaged.

Christ's Mission since its founding in New York by converted priest James A. O'Connor has helped close to three hundred former priests to find this new and living way of salvation. Most of them have devoted the remaining years of their lives to Evangelical and Protestant Church work in the different denominations. Every effort is made by the Catholic Church authorities to keep the Catholic people from all contact with such men. The obvious reason for this determined policy of ostracizing ex-priests is the fear of the change that would take place if 'free' priests were allowed to retain scope for religious work among the Catholic people.

Priests who attempted such reform in the Catholic Church in the centuries preceding the Protestant Reformation were not only degraded, but also depriv-

ed of civil rights and made liable to imprisonment and
death. Legal marriage for them was then impossible,
since the penalties decreed by the laws of the Church
were carried out by the civil power. Yet the most out-
standing figures in the history of religious reform
were rebel priests of the Roman Catholic Church:
Huss, Wycliffe, Savonarola, Bruno, Luther, Erasmus,
Knox and a host of others. Mention should be made
also of those who remained within the Catholic Church
and tried to reform it from within: Francis of Assisi,
Thomas à Kempis, Theresa and Catherine of Siena.

Mussolini's Fascism restored some of the
medieval disabilities against priests who leave the
priesthood. Article 7 of the Lateran Concordat between Mussolini and Pope Pius XI in 1929 deprived
ex-priests in Italy of public employment in any oc-
cupation that would bring them into contact with the
people. In modern democratic countries ex-priests enjoy the full liberties of free-born citizens. They may
marry, have legitimate children and obtain employment in private or public business.

But even in democratic countries such as the
United States, ex-priests are still denied access to their
former people if they try to help them understand
the true teaching of Christianity. As long as they
remained within the confines of the Church no obstacle
was placed in their way of preaching to the people the
prescribed doctrines manufactured by the Roman
theologians. As soon as they come to a knowledge of
the true Gospel way of salvation, they are hindered in
every possible way from making that known. All the
premeditated arts of false propaganda are employed

to vilify and blacken the name and reputation of a former priest. The opprobrious names of renegade, apostate, Judas, are applied to him in order to poison the minds of the simple Catholic people against him— although they were once obliged to pay him homage as God's chosen minister of their salvation.

Many find it difficult to understand why so many young men and women choose to devote themselves for life to the rigorous system of the Roman Catholic Church as priests and nuns. Getting into the service of the Church, however, is not difficult; getting out after it is too late is the real problem. Young boys and girls are recruited at an age when the idealism of ad- olescence is strong in all youth. The Catholic Church seeks candidates for its personnel during the years from sixteen to eighteen, when spiritual ideals are strongest, but illusive and superficial. It is the age when youth feels the urge for self-sacrifice. Like the carrier-wave of a radio transmitter, the idealistic urge will accept whatever is placed upon it, and will carry it direct to the desired goal.

It is not then foreseen that this youthful idealism will cool to freezing at the touch of the hard realities of the priesthood and convent life. By the time this disillusionment comes, the priest and nun are no long- er free to make it known. The anguish of heart and crucifixion of mind that follow this spiritual disillu- sionment must be kept sealed within the breast. This anguish is not lessened by the necessary outward show of contentment and perplexed resignation.

During their years in the seminary as students for the priesthood Catholic boys generally treat lightly

the prospect of their future celibate life. No contact
with girls is allowed them during the school year,
though some of them in the United States go out with
girls during vacation time. In the seminaries in Rome,
however, they are kept to a strict barracks life all year
round, and are forbidden ever to go out on the street
alone. At night they are securely locked into their
cells. They have a hazy notion that the oil of ordination has some prophylactic quality that will resolve
the human weakness of the seminary student into a
priestly fortitude that will make him proof for ever
after against all the attacks of the world, the flesh and
the devil.

In the American College in Rome a ceremony is
performed on the eve of ordinations that would be
amusing were it not so pathetic and taken so seriously
by the students. Those destined to receive the order
of subdiaconate on the morrow—after which they will
be bound by the law of celibacy—are entertained at a
kind of *agape*, or love feast, prepared for them by
their senior deacons. Toward the end of the meal, the
prospective celibates stand in line holding aloft a gob-
let of sparkling Frascati wine. Then, after a tragi-
comic oration by the presiding deacon, they solemnly
pronounce together the toast of the occasion: *"To the
girl who would have been my wife!"*

The Roman Catholic Church spares neither pains
nor money to make its priests well fitted for their
task. Although its priests are often considered lacking
in refinement and modern learning, their knowledge
of some of the Latin classics, scholastic philosophy and

Roman theology gives them a standing in the community that is the boast of their congregations. They are trained for just one purpose: the preservation and further aggrandizement of the structure of the Roman Catholic Church. To many today it must seem a cruel and selfish policy, as well as a waste of effort, thus to cut and polish the rough diamond and then cast it aside when it has served this one purpose. Forbidden legal marriage and children, priests cannot pass on their personal, physical or mental qualities, nor the result of any literary achievement to generations of their own blood. Great indeed must be the fear of the havoc which such perpetuation of knowledge and free intellectual effort in a second or third generation of priests' children would cause to the organization of the Catholic Church. The Church might indeed be the loser. On the other hand, there would be the gain among the Catholic people of a much needed uplift, social, intellectual and spiritual.

It is not for spiritual reasons that the Roman Catholic Church has for so many centuries denied legitimate marriage to its priests. Those in power have always known that it is only the legality of the marriage relation that can be denied them, and that the custom of clerical concubinage, with resultant generations of illegitimate offspring, has always taken its place. Loss of centralized power and property titles, disruption of its authoritarian system of government, would have been the result if these generations of priests' children in the past had been legalized. Clerical concubinage has thus been tolerated in preference to this loss of undisputed power centered in Rome.

The children of a priest in the past had the right to call him 'Father' only in the spiritual sense of the word. The illegitimate sons of popes, cardinals and bishops, however, were often enabled to rise to high positions in the Church and the State. Several popes were themselves sons and grandsons of other popes and high Church dignitaries. My researches among the collections of papal bulls reveal that concubinage among the clergy in Europe was so prevalent that it was necessary to regulate the practice by law—lest clerical concubinage itself should ever become a legal right. I was surprised to discover how many of these papal bulls relate to concubinage among the priests in my native Ireland, where the simple Catholic people would be shocked to hear any one connect their priests with the urge of sex.

Thus the priests no less than the people they teach are made the victims of the deceits of Roman Catholicism.

CHAPTER FIFTEEN

THE TYRANNY OF PRIESTLY CELIBACY

ONLY THOSE PRIESTS who leave the ranks of the Roman priesthood are free to speak their minds about celibacy. Many even then hesitate to do so, for fear of scandalizing those they left behind them. But some, such as Father Chiniquy, Père Hyacinthe and others, considered it a duty to prove how harmful to the cause of Christ has been this false position into which Roman Catholic priests are forced with regard to sex and marriage. In the first place it is unscriptural, for the apostle Paul (1 *Tim.* 4: 3) warns against those who depart from the faith and give heed to "doctrines of devils," by "forbidding to marry and commanding to abstain from meats." And in the preceding chapter he tells Timothy that even *"a bishop must be a man of one wife."*

Père Hyacinthe, French priest and famed preacher of Notre Dame in Paris, after his conversion compared the wounds inflicted upon the Christian Church by the Roman papacy to the wounds in the crucified body of Christ. "Behold ye bishops," he exclaimed, "the Bride of Christ pierced, like Him, by five wounds!" He likens the first wound in the right hand of Christ, the hand that carries the light of truth, to the darkening of the Word of God—the denial of the Gospel to the people. The wound in the left hand is the abuse of hierarchical power. But he calls the wound in the very heart of Christ's Church the forced celibacy of the clergy, "suffered most by those (the priests themselves) who dare least to speak of it."

I am breaking no confidences when I assert that it is sheer pretense to say that this forced celibacy contributes in any way to the personal sanctification of priests. The sole benefit to be had from it is the strengthening of the organizational structure of the Church. Hitler, in his *Mein Kampf*, was uncannily accurate in figuring out and stressing this. *"This particular significance of celibacy,"* he says, *"is not recognized by most people."* Holding up the organization of the Roman Catholic Church as a model example for his Nazi followers, he goes on to say (p. 643):

"Here the Catholic Church can be looked upon as a model example. In the celibacy of its priests roots the compulsion to draw the future generations of the clergy, instead of from its own ranks, again and again from the broad masses of the people. . . . It is the origin of the incredibly vigorous power that inhabits this age-old institution. This gigantic host of clerical dignitaries, by uninterruptedly supplementing itself from the lowest layers of the nations, preserves not only its instinctive bond with the people's world of sentiment, but it also assures itself of a sum of energy and active force which in such a form will forever be present only in the broad masses of the people. From this results the astounding youthfulness of this giant organism, its spiritual pliability and its steel-like will power."

This fulsome praise by Hitler of the unnatural law of priestly celibacy should reveal to Americans

how insincere are the pious protestations of deep concern of Catholic spokesmen for the "sacredness of the
individual personality."   Hitler, whose *Mein Kampf*
was ghost-written by a Roman Catholic priest, proves
that the Catholic Church sacrifices the most natural
human instincts of its own clergy to the strengthening
of its "giant organism and its steel-like will power."

The real shame and tyranny of priestly celibacy,
as Père Hyacinthe rightly remarks, is the necessity
to which its victims are forced of hiding the real facts
of it from the public.   It is unnecessary for me to say
how many priests fail to live up to the harsh requirements of this unnatural law.   Priests as a group are
little different from other men of like temperament
and profession.   Their weakness in sex matters is no
less than those of other men of corresponding position
and education.   It may safely be said, in fact, that
the sex urge in priests is even stronger because of the
denial to them of the cleansing effects of legal marriage.   Roman Catholic priests do not have the advantage of active business men, whose sex tendencies
are generally normalized by physical absorption in
daily labor, unremitting cares of family life and
harassing financial affairs.   They lead a very seden-
tary life, are freely supplied with an exceptionally
good table and other bodily comforts, and are officials
of a religion which does not prohibit indulgence in the
copious use of alcoholic stimulants.

Similar to so many other man-made regulations
of the Roman Catholic Church, priestly celibacy entails many contradictions, much deceit, and often
leads to complete spiritual shipwreck of its victims.   In

the first place, there is the convenient confusion between the words *celibacy* and *chastity*. To the ordinary people these are made to appear identical, and both Catholics and Protestants are led to believe that every Roman Catholic priest must take "vows of chastity" before ordination. This confusion serves as an easy defense of the organization of the Catholic Church in more ways than one. In particular, it enables the defenders of the Church to cast a slur on priests who leave the priesthood and subsequently get married as having "broken their vows of chastity." This is pure fiction. Only the very small percentage of priests who belong to the religious orders take an explicit vow of chastity. Of the 40,000 Roman Catholic priests in the United States, fully 80 per cent are 'secular' priests who serve in parishes and who do not take any vow of chastity at ordination.

At ordination these secular priests merely signify that they accept the Church's condition for ordination *that they will not get legally married*. They take no vow of chastity, that is, they make no explicit promise to refrain from sexual relations. Cadets at West Point and Annapolis are bound by similar regulations. Much more, in fact, is said about chastity by a Protestant Episcopal bishop when ordaining ministers to that Church which permits them to marry as they please, either before or after ordination.

In other words, one can continue to be celibate without necessarily being chaste. A Roman Catholic priest ceases to be celibate in the eyes of his Church only by contracting marriage by permission of the Church. No amount of sexual relations will affect

his celibacy. Sometimes it happens that a priest takes
the law into his own hands and secretly contracts
legal marriage before a Protestant minister or a civil
judge. In such a case he would still be counted as
celibate by the Catholic Church, since it does not recognize any power in a Protestant minister or a civil
judge to join in matrimony those whom it has banned
from marriage.

The absurd consequences of the Catholic Church's
law of priestly celibacy may be seen from the regulations governing the pardon of priests who sin by
sexual relationship without getting married, compared to those who flout the Church's law of celibacy
and contract legal marriage before a Protestant minister or a civil judge. Pardon for sexual irregularities of priests outside marriage, whether adultery or
fornication, can easily be had at any time by confession to any ordinary fellow-priest. On the other
hand, absolution (with accompanying severe penalties) for a priest who gets legally married can be obtained for him only by recourse to the pope himself.
Furthermore, to obtain such pardon a priest would
be obliged to forsake his wife. What is regarded as
the real crime in this latter case is not the actual marriage act, but the defiance of the law of celibacy.

Most dishonest of all is the use of the law of celibacy against priests who resign from the priesthood
and subsequently get married. Against them is made
the unfair accusation that they left just to get married, that they are so many 'Judases' who betray God
and the Church merely to satisfy their base passions.
The truth of the matter is, as is well known to all

priests, that the priesthood provides a safe and convenient cloak for those who choose to lead an irregular sex life, whereas the restrictions and burdens of married life which an ex-priest chooses are a deterrent to such extra-marital sex irregularities. Nor do all priests who leave the priesthood get married afterwards. Many of them cannot afford to do so, and some are already past marriageable age.

Forced celibacy in any Christian Church is not only unscriptural but out-moded in democratic countries. The Roman Catholic Church was formerly admitted to be the sole law-maker for marriages of all Christians. But the will of the people in democratic countries has now placed that right in the hands of the civil authorities. The law of clerical celibacy, with its denial of legal marriage to priests, is now no longer binding. It has continued in the Roman Catholic Church only because its authorities have taken unfair advantage of the false idea it has fostered among the credulous people that priests are forbidden to marry by the law of God.

The fact is adroitly concealed from the submissive Catholic people that celibacy is merely a regulation of Church law, and that it is no sin or shame before God for a priest to get properly married. Roman Catholics will not believe that the apostle Peter had a wife, even though this fact is mentioned in the Gospel of Matthew. Neither will they believe that, when it was expedient to do so, the Catholic Church released large numbers of priests from this law. The Vatican's concordat with Napoleon, for instance, ratified the marriages of those priests who took the oath to the Constitution after the French Revolution of 1789, by which the legality of the marriages of priests was recognized. Talleyrand, the Roman Catholic Bishop of Autun who became Napoleon's great statesman, took the law into his own hands and got married. The pope was willing to ratify the bishop's marriage in return for other political concessions by Napoleon. Just because Napoleon did not consider it a good bargain for him, the pope spited him and withheld his permission for Talleyrand's marriage. Roman Catholic people also find it difficult to believe that in New York and other American cities today parish priests of the Ruthenian and other Greek Catholic rites have wives and families.

In my book, *The Soul of a Priest*, I have told of the sad spectacles I met, in all parts of the world in which I travelled as a priest, of the ruined lives of so many fine young priests who through no fault of their own were unable to bear up against this harsh law of celibacy. It has been well said that marriage cleanses a man, and these young priests would have been cleansed of the annoyance and frustration of sex by normal marriage relations. A loving wife and the joy of legitimate children in a happy home life would have filled them with vigor and spiritual zeal. Even more important, these would have saved them from the inevitable indulgence in alcoholic liquor to which many priests are driven as a poor substitute for their God-given, natural rights in marriage.

The bishops know this well. So does the pope and his Roman counsellors. But they prefer to wreck the souls and bodies of the priests in order to sustain the "giant organism" and "steel-like will power" of its organization that Hitler so greatly admired and imitated. They take the fresh young man, the rough, uncut diamond, use him for the ends of their organization and then cast him aside when his usefulness is gone, and then begin again on others. The "particular significance of celibacy" in their regimented, Nazi-like organization, which Hitler discovered as "not recognized by most people," lies in the fact that the second and third generation of priests' children would threaten its totalitarian structure, as well as its enormous wealth and secrets. To preserve these the individual souls of its priests are cruelly sacrificed.

There is an angle to this law of priestly celibacy in the Roman Catholic Church that does not make sense to Protestants, as it did to Hitler. The loss to Roman Catholic countries because of the prohibition of legal marriage to its priests has been clearly shown by men like Professor Albert Wigham of Columbia University in New York, and by Havelock Ellis in England. Their investigations prove that the children of Protestant clergymen in England, America and Evangelical countries of Europe are proportionately much superior in intellectual and scientific achievement than those of all other professions. Their tabulations show that one member out of every twenty families of Protestant clergymen is to be found listed in *Who's Who* compared to one out of every 800 families of farmers, and only one out of every 2,000 families of shopkeepers and tradesmen.

Priests and nuns are the cream of the Roman Catholic population in every country. Yet they leave no such superior progeny behind them as is to be found in Protestant countries. Even in the United States, the selection of the best youths for a celibate priesthood in the Catholic Church is sure to have harmful effects on future generations, especially if the number of Roman Catholics increases to any great extent.

It seems senseless, on the one hand, that the Roman Catholic Church insists on a tremendous increase of children among its poor and uneducated classes by unrelenting opposition to birth control, and, on the other hand, denies legal marriage and legitimate children to its millions of priests, nuns, monks and teaching brothers. These can produce children only surreptitiously—or employ the very methods of birth control which they are obliged to deny to the laity.

An absurd consequence of this denial of marriage to priests is the false idea, especially among Irish Catholics and the peasant peoples of southern Europe, that marriage and the priesthood are entirely incompatible. They believe that the priesthood eliminates in some miraculous way even the physical possibility of the marriage relation in one so endowed. A Protestant minister, of course, cannot be thus supernaturally affected, since he has no power of the priesthood. These credulous people scarcely allow their minds to think of their priests as having even the ordinary natural bodily functions of other men.

This was well illustrated to me by an Irish priest by the name of Frank Kelly in Capetown. He told the story purposely at his own father's expense to prove the super-physical picture that Irish people have in their minds of their priests. His father was a store keeper in Waterford in the south of Ireland and often engaged the local Protestant minister in theological discussions. One day the conversation turned on the question of the marriage of priests. "Sure an' that could never be," Mr. Kelly objected to the Protestant minister. " 'Twould be aginst all law of God and man!"

"But my dear Mr. Kelly," the minister retorted, "in the Holy Bible Paul tells Timothy that even a bishop must be a man of one wife. Why then not also a priest?"

"Faith an' bigorra," the priest's father indignantly answered, "that may be in *your* Bible, but 'tis sure not in mine!"

When the minister inquired if he had a Bible at home, Mr. Kelly heatedly replied: "Sure I have! We Catholics can have a Bible as well as Protestants."

They agreed to go to his house and find out if the passage in question was in the Catholic Bible. Arrived there, Mr. Kelly proudly took down the family Bible from a shelf, carefully dusted it and handed it to the Protestant minister confident that he would be disappointed in his search. The minister quickly turned to I *Tim.* 3: 2 and read aloud: "A bishop must be the husband of one wife . . ." He then handed the book to Mr. Kelly who adjusted his spectacles and read the passage for himself. Suspicious of some trick on the part of the minister he turned to the fly-leaf, to convince himself it was really his own Bible by the record of all the Kelly baptisms written on it. He then removed his spectacles, carefully wiped them, and again read the passage aloud for himself. Finally, convinced but still unbelieving, he closed the book with a snap, threw it on the table and exclaimed:

"Faith, an' 'tis Saint Paul ought to be ashamed of himself!"

CHAPTER SIXTEEN

BY WHAT AUTHORITY . . . ?

THE PROBLEM of how the grace of salvation is
dispensed to sinners in Christian theology is generally discounted by people of the world as of purely
academic interest only to theologians. This is not true.
I believe it to be a very practical and important matter, since it has had a direct bearing upon the conduct
of political and economic affairs in the history of
western civilization for the past fifteen hundred years.
It is closely connected with the problem of free will,
which has been used as the yardstick by popes and
kings to determine the measure of control they considered necessary to restrict the thoughts, actions and
aspirations of men. It is basic to the great question
that has agitated mankind of all ages: by what authority must men be ruled?

Prior to the Protestant Reformation, this control
was exercised exclusively by the double-headed divine
sovereignty of Pope and Emperor, as the only channel
through which the grace of salvation and a measure
of freedom were allowed. It was sustained by the
accepted principle that men are free to work out
neither their own spiritual salvation, nor their own
ethical business code, in keeping with any private
opinion about God or their choice of a power to govern
them. They were left free only to sin, by disobeying
the dictates of the established human authority in

Church and State—free also to suffer the liabilities
of its punitive force.

In fact, it was precisely this power to punish
which gave to this dual authority its very reason for
existence.   And since its power to punish and condemn was so essential to sustain its existence, it was
very important that men should be left sufficiently
free to sin against its dictates.

Upon its peculiar teaching about grace and free
will is based the Roman Catholic theory of world sovereignty, which was overthrown in the countries of
northern Europe by Luther and Calvin.   These reformers completely reversed the whole process in the
conduct of religion, politics and economics.   For they
abolished obedience to unwarranted human authority, and threw mankind back directly upon the will
and power of deity.   Thenceforth they made it so
that men were free, on the one hand, of all human
dictatorship in spiritual matters, but without any
freedom, on the other hand, as regards the will of God.
They decreed that men are rigidly bound to God,
that those who are good are good by compulsion of
God, and that those who are not good are evil by mis-
fortune.

The effect of this change in theology was immediately felt in the political order, and led to the constitution of modern States (before the rise of ultra-mod-
ern Fascist and Communist dictatorships), wherein
it was laid down that no temporal authority could be
recognized unless it was freely delegated by the individual choice of the people.   This was in keeping
with the principle, which the reformers re-discovered

in the New Testament, of the power of God within man. They held that the grace of salvation is a free gift of God, and is not merited by human works. God, being the only sovereign and free agent, cannot be either forced or cajoled, by pope or prince, to bestow it upon anybody. Those upon whom He chooses to bestow His gift are not only freely chosen by Him, but have not the ability to choose not to accept it.

It was this cutting of the individual adrift from control by a corporate, totalitarian system of religion that set the trend of western civilization toward freedom and individualistic effort in all phases of life. It acted as a great force for the disintegration of all centralized human control. It glorified the independent efforts of each one as the necessary incentive for progress in all things. Ever since the sixteenth century, it has been hailed by the exponents of liberalism not only as a scientific, but also a biologic necessity.

The defenders of Roman Catholicism still regard it, on the contrary, as a virulent disease contracted by western civilization at the time of the Protestant Reformation, and which has taken, not the usual four weeks, but four centuries to run its course. The first serious threat against this new order that came out of the Reformation happened in our time, by the rise to power in Europe of Mussolini and Hitler. As was to be expected, the Vatican was the first to rush into agreement with them, first with Mussolini by the Lateran Pacts of 1929, and then with Hitler by the concordat signed July 20, 1933, by Cardinal Eugenio Pacelli (later Pope Pius XII) and Franz von Papen, shortly after the Nazis came to power. Lewis Mumford, in his *Faith for Living* (p. 160), confirmed my findings in 1940, that "*the betrayal of the Christian world, very plainly, took place in 1929, in the concordat that was made between Mussolini and the Pope.*"

During the four hundred years from Calvin's time to the rise of Fascism and Nazism, the Roman Catholic Church resisted the Protestant teaching about grace with all the force at its disposal. The Jesuits, sworn to their plan of counter-Reformation, were fully aware that the Roman Catholic Church would cease to exist all together if it were to admit that men could be saved and governed without the intervention and control of a hierarchical Church and State. The power of all dictators, religious and political, depends upon the weakness of those subject to them. Despotic human authority requires that the masses of the people be taught that they are hopelessly weak, free and prone to sin, so that the dictators in Church and State may be able to save (and punish) them. Above all, they must be taught that they cannot save themselves and, being cut off from God, they cannot look to Him to obtain directly from Him, and through Christ, the grace of salvation.

Of the utmost importance, therefore, for the continuance of Catholic power is the teaching that the grace of salvation is irrevocably confined in the controlling channels of the seven sacraments of the Roman Catholic Church, and administered solely by its priests. To be resisted at all costs is the Protestant teaching, that this grace falls freely, like dew from heaven, upon all alike.

More blood than grace, however, has flowed from
this claim of the Roman Catholic Church to have the
monopoly of dispensing salvation to all men.   There
is no evidence of those white and lustrous streams of
grace that the Church of Rome has always boasted
to be able to generate and pour into the souls of men.
In evidence, instead, have been the torrents of red
blood that have deluged the nations of Christendom
as a result of the wars and strifes occasioned by its
efforts to force the nations of Europe to recognize its
unscriptural claim.

A sea of ink has also been spilled over the techni-
cal question of the nature and operation of this grace
of salvation.   Furious debate divided the Roman theologians within the Catholic Church itself.   But the
strife was not confined within the walls of the theological schools and universities.   It was applied to the
lives of the people and used in the political intrigues
of the nations with the result that the earth was
soaked with the blood of the Christian people in whose
behalf the blood of Christ was shed to the last drop.
It would seem that the Roman Catholic Church, having monopolized the teaching about salvation by the
blood of Christ, so utterly distorted that teaching to
its own advantage that it became necessary that the
grace of salvation could not continue to flow into the
souls of men without a corresponding flow of the blood
of those thus redeemed.   This blood-letting as a consequence of the Roman Catholic Church's persistent
bid for religious world supremacy, far from diminish-
ing in modern times, has increased in intensity, as the
two world wars in our own generation have proved.

Till the time of the Protestant Reformation, only a few bold spirits within the Roman Catholic Church itself dared to dispute the theory and practice of grace as an external force that could be granted or withheld at the whim of those in power. These few were easily disposed of by the rack and the stake. Even the very ashes of their burnt bodies were scattered on the water of swift-flowing rivers which carried them out to sea. It was thus thought that their spirit of protest would not remain, even in the memory of men, to disturb the Church's absolute possession of the souls of all men. After the Reformation this bloodletting of heretics became a sacred duty in defense of the Catholic Church's monopoly of grace, and was undertaken with zest and profit. The flow of blood rather than of grace became the principal business of the Church of Rome.

Today in America, Protestant opposition to this Roman Catholic claim to be the only institution with the monopoly of this grace of salvation is being fought no less relentlessly, but by less violent means—by a kind of warfare of nerves. Protestants are being frightened into believing that all the crime, religious indifference, especially the spread of atheistic communism, are the direct result of their rejection of the Roman Catholic Church as the true and only religion of Christ. From pulpit and platform, through the secular press and continuous radio broadcasts, as well as in mountains of Catholic literature, spokesmen for the Church of Rome condemn even the sacred institutions of American democracy as Godless and evil because they deny this claim of the Catholic Church.

Everything wrong with our American Protestant
culture, they assert, is directly traceable to our rejection of the Catholic Church's monopoly of the grace
of salvation.

This barrage of blame and abuse of everything
Protestant is slowly having effect. Doubts are being entertained about the wisdom of American public-
school education, of the heretofore cherished principle of the separation of Church and State, of keeping Roman clerical influence out of politics, labor relations, and in general of what is called the growing
'secularization' of American life. The new scientific
teachings of psychiatry and psychology, of modern
medicine, marriage and sex, and especially of the deterministic behaviorism now generally accepted in
opposition to Roman Catholic medieval teaching on
these subjects, are violently attacked as leading us
away from God. A few people prominent in public
life, such as Mrs. Clare Boothe Luce, Senator Wagner
and young Henry Ford, have been inveigled into joining the Roman Catholic Church by the blandishments of
Monsignor Fulton J. Sheen and have become ardent
disciples in his crusade against Protestantism. It has
been made to appear that the only way to sanity and
salvation is to fall into line and obtain from Msgr.
Sheen a ticket-of-entry into the kingdom of heaven.

Is it true that America has become a wayward
nation because it has continued to follow Protestant
rather than Roman Catholic teaching about the grace
of salvation? I would say this is true only in so far
as people have been falsely led to believe that Protestant teaching and culture must be judged by the ex-

cesses that we see around us in American life today. So-called secularization of American society, it is true, can be traced to our constitutional principle of separation of Church and State; so also lack of religious instruction in our public schools. The freedoms and liberties guaranteed to and enjoyed by all alike in the United States are sure to lead to excesses in some particulars. The teaching of deterministic behaviorism, though it is the logical consequence of Calvin's doctrine of grace and free will, may sometimes lead to a denial of salvation and the need to be spiritually born again.

On the other hand, I find that wrong conclusions arrived at by the modern school of behaviorists, far from proving Protestant Christianity wrong on the question of the grace of salvation, actually prove that Calvin was right. If the scientific findings of the behaviorists are correct, that what we are and do in life is all fixed and predetermined in the womb, then a spiritual re-birth and a separate life of the spirit become an absolute necessity. They prove beyond a doubt the truth of Christ's own teaching: "Ye must be born again."

Monsignor Sheen and his satellites frighten Protestants into the Roman Catholic Church by making them believe that unless you become a Roman Catholic you must accept the conclusions of the behaviorists; that if you insist upon separation of Church and State you must be in favor of the complete secularization of education and of all life; that if you continue to reject the religious dictatorship of the Roman

Catholic Church you will finally end up by joining the
atheistic communists.   This is pure Jesuit sophistry.
You can agree with the findings of the behaviorists
and the communists without accepting their conclusions.   There is no need to follow the behaviorists
because they have discovered that our moods and mannerisms are predetermined for us by the quality of
our thyroid, pituitary, adrenal, pineal and other bits
of tissue, that the small margin of free will we have
can be compared to that of a little dog tied to a tree.
Calvin four hundred years ago reminded us of this,
and he learned it from Augustine, who in turn learned
it from the New Testament.   Neither is there need
to follow the communists just because they have discovered that every man is entitled to enough to eat
and the wherewith to be clothed and sheltered.   For
this again is good New Testament teaching.

The newest methods of modern democratic education are as old as early Christian Evangelical teaching.   Both repudiate and by-pass the hair-splitting,
deductive rationalizing of Roman Catholic medieval
philosophy.   Both are experimental, pragmatic, and
depend on facts, not mere theories.   Modern, so-called
Godless, education admits a thing to be true if it
works.   Evangelical Christianity says likewise that
religion is true if it works.   The religion that changes
the heart of a man, that turns him from a sinner into
a saint, that is true religion.   The kind that bases
everything about sin and God upon what casuistic
theologians have dogmatized into Christianity from
their academic chairs is what Christ condemned by
reference to the gnat and the camel in *Matt.* 23:24.

"By their fruits you shall know them," is also true Christian methodology.

Many in America today are deceived by Monsignor Sheen and his disciples into believing that the Roman Catholic Church is in favor of freedom because it is in favor of free will. The opposite is the case. It is opposed to freedom precisely because it advocates free will. Those who deny free will, on the other hand, are the advocates of freedom. Nor is there any paradox involved in saying so. For freedom is not something that is given to you. It is an effect, not a cause; something that develops as a consequence of a fixed state of being. By being fixed and bound to God's sovereign will as regards our spiritual salvation, we are fully liberated in all things, both spiritual and material, from bondage to men. "Whom the Son makes free is free indeed." We are made free by being tied to God.

All tyrannies and dictatorships have been based upon freedom of the will. Hitler, faithful admirer and imitator of everything Catholic, glorified free will like the Roman Catholic Church in order to establish his Nazi tyranny. All education in the Roman Catholic Church centers around the training of the will. Education to the Roman Catholic Church, as to Hitler and his like, is solely for *formation,* not *information.* Free will is a fiction by which they deny freedom and regiment and condition action and reaction. In this way men become slaves in bondage to other men.

Calvin, Luther and other Protestant reformers are hated by the Roman Catholic Church because they taught, according to true Christian doctrine, that man is not free to earn his own salvation, that it is a free gift of God. Freed thus in the spirit a man is free also in the things of the body. *"For the law of the spirit of life in Christ Jesus hath made me free from the law of sin and death"* (*Rom.* 8: 2). A man who is born again in the spirit becomes a son of God, and therefore can never again be a slave of man.

To the teaching of Calvin and other priest-reformers on free will and grace we owe our freedoms in modern democratic countries. Only by resisting the contrary teaching on grace and free will by the Roman Catholic Church can we preserve those freedoms.

CHAPTER SEVENTEEN

GOD IS NOT A BACKSTAIRS POLITICIAN

I FIND IT most difficult to convince Roman Catholic people that Christ has won for sinners the right of direct access to God. They always fall back on what their priests have taught them, that to obtain mercy and forgiveness they must cajole some saint, some close and favored friend of God to intercede for them. The most powerful intercessor of them all is Mary, since she, they say, is the actual mother of God.

A very sincere and devout Catholic woman once put it to me in the following way. "If you wanted an interview with President Truman," she argued, "you would have to go first to some one else, his mother or some of his political friends, and ask them to intercede for you with the President and arrange for you to see him." My answer was, of course, that that may be true as far as President Truman is concerned. "But it so happens," I told her, "that President Truman is not God."

This belief of Roman Catholics is in accord with their Church's peculiar teaching that Jesus Christ brought only *justice* on earth, and that Mary and the other saints must be looked to for *mercy*. "Ye know very well, venerable brethren," Pope Pius IX declares in one of his encyclicals, "that the whole of our confidence is placed in the most Holy Virgin, since God has placed in Mary the fullness of all good, *that accordingly we may know that if there is any hope in us, if any grace, if any salvation, it redounds to us from her.*"

From this extravagance it follows, in the eyes of Roman Catholics who are taught in this way, that Mary and the saints have even more power to save than Christ. They come to believe that the saints can get them into heaven, literally, by the backstairs, even if they die before a priest can come to forgive them their sins. Saint Joseph, for instance, has been officially proclaimed by the Catholic Church as the *"Patron of a Happy Death."* This special work is given to him because he was the foster-father of Jesus Christ and because he died before Jesus left home to begin His ministry. He therefore had Our Lord and the Virgin Mary at his deathbed. As the husband of Mary, Joseph is believed to be very powerful as an intercessor with Jesus Christ, and can actually get sinners into heaven at the last minute even if they die without a priest to absolve them.

Priests go to extraordinary lengths to convince their congregations that devotion to Saint Joseph is the surest guarantee sinners can have of getting to heaven. They picture him as heaven's most powerful 'politician' who can obtain any favor he wants from God. I remember how a priest in Naples, Italy, once proved this in a sermon to his congregation. Here is the story he told (which is true in every detail according to what Catholics are taught about heaven, Jesus, Mary, Joseph, Saint Peter, Saint Michael and others there) :

One day the Archangel Michael, the policeman of heaven, came to Saint Peter at the golden gates and said: "Look here, Peter! How is it that there are so many scoundrels in heaven who have no right to be here? Heaven is swarming with sinners who don't deserve a place even in Purgatory."

"Don't blame me, Michael," Peter replied. "Everyone knows my reputation as guardian of the heavenly gates. You know I would never let even a Pope get in unless I'm sure first that all his sins are forgiven and that he has served his full time in Purgatory. But since you've asked me a straight question I'll give you a straight answer, if you'll come with me after I've closed up the gates for the night."

They met as appointed and Peter led the way around the outer walls of the Celestial City to where the house of the 'Holy Family' was situated, high up against one of the battlements, and from the back window of which the Holy Family—Mary, Joseph and the infant Jesus—could look down and see everything that takes place on earth.

It was a bright moonlit night and Peter drew Michael down behind some shrubbery and told him to wait and see what would happen. After a little while, they heard what seemed like pebbles being thrown against the window overlooking the wall. In less than a minute the window was opened, and a rope was let down and pulled up again. At the end of the rope was one of the disreputable sinners whom Michael had complained about.

They waited until the sinner was hauled in and the window shut. "Now," said Peter triumphantly to the amazed Archangel, "There's your answer!"

Next morning early, Michael, dressed in his best official uniform, and with a very determined look on his face, knocked at the door of the Holy Family's house. Mary opened the door and called to Joseph and the Child Jesus to welcome their distinguished visitor. He took a seat and in a tone of the sternest dignity turned to Joseph and said: "Joseph, I've found out what has been going on here every night, and I would fail in my sacred duty if I did not tell you that your practice of getting sinners into heaven by your back window must stop at once!"

"I'm sorry, Your Highness," Joseph replied with a guilty look, "but I'm publicized on earth as the last refuge of dying sinners. I've furthermore been proclaimed 'Patron of the Universal Church,' and I've solemnly promised to get poor sinners into heaven by hook or by crook who are faithful in their devotion to me during life. I simply can't refuse their appeals and let them go to hell. My position and reputation as husband of Mary and the foster-father of Jesus Christ are at stake."

Michael rose from his chair, and drawing himself up to his full archangelic height, decisively replied: ·

"There can be no exceptions to the eternal and immutable justice of the Almighty God whose stern commands I am appointed to carry out to the letter. Since the day I hurled Lucifer and his rebellious angels from these same ramparts of heaven, I've been

*entrusted with the duty of keeping sinners out of it,
and seeing that the laws of the Almighty are rigidly
enforced."*

"In that case," Joseph meekly replied, "I can no
longer stay in heaven. I must go elsewhere and try to
keep my promisees to poor dying sinners."

As Joseph moved to the door, Mary ran to him
and clutched his arm. Turning to the unbending Archangel, she said: "Joseph is my lawful husband, and if
he goes I go too, and then there will be no Queen in
heaven!" Michael was taken back at this thought, and
tried to find words to meet this unexpected situation.
But before he could think of anything appropriate to
say, the Child Jesus spoke and said: *"And if my
mother goes I will have to go too, and then you'll have
no God in heaven either!"*

This was too much, even for the Archangel
Michael, and knowing himself defeated, he bowed
himself out of the house with as much dignity as he
could muster.

"And that is the reason why," this Neapolitan
priest told his listeners, *"no one who practices devotion to Saint Joseph during life will fail to get into
heaven."*

There are some, even non-Catholics, who will say
this is a very *realistic* and *human* way of preaching
to ignorant people who cannot read and write or understand the things of God in the words of the Gospel.
But is this sufficient excuse for the Roman Catholic
Church which has been the sole, undisputed teacher
of Christian people for more than fifteen centuries?
The Roman Catholic Church insists to this day on be-

ing the sole interpreter of the Bible, its Pope the infallible mouthpiece of God. It could as easily have taught the people the truth from the New Testament which records Christ as saying (*John* 10: 9): "*I am the door: by me if any man enter in, he shall be saved, and shall go in and out, and find pasture.*" Or again (*John* 14: 6): "*I am the way, and the truth, and the life: no man cometh unto the Father but by me.*" Or again (*Acts* 4:12): "*Neither is there salvation in any other, for there is no other name under heaven given among men whereby we must be saved.*"

But doing so would have meant the scrapping of its many shrines, saint-devotions and novenas, which are financially so profitable.

CHAPTER EIGHTEEN

THE BONDAGE OF DOING

ROMAN CATHOLIC TEACHING rests upon the principle that eternal salvation depends upon the works performed by the hands of its priests. This principle is expressed by the phrase, *ex opere operato* (literally, "because of the work that is worked"), coined by the theologians in Rome to convey the belief that the grace of salvation can be made to flow into the souls of men only through the works performed upon them by validly ordained priests of the Roman Catholic Church.

They have another phrase to complement this: *ex opere operantis* ("because of the work of the worker"), which means that the individual must also earn his salvation by works of penance and mortification as commanded by the Church. But these works of the individual are of no avail without the works that are worked upon him by the priest. Both of these kinds of works, however, are contradictory of the new and living way of salvation as clearly set forth in the New Testament: "*Not by works of righteousness which we have done, but according to His mercy He saved us, by the washing of regeneration, and renewing of the Holy Ghost.*" (*Titus* 3 : 5).

Of prime importance, therefore, to the young priest setting out from the seminary to begin his ministry are his anointed and consecrated hands. Many hundreds of newly-ordained priests, with the oil of ordination scarcely dry on their hands, enter each year on the active work of the Roman Catholic priesthood in the United States. Pious men and devout women and young girls love to kiss these freshly-anointed hands. For they believe that these hands will carry the body of Jesus Christ to countless thousands of the faithful, and that they will be the actual instruments for the signing away, by absolution in confession, the crimes of men against God and the many mortal sins committed against the laws of the Roman Catholic Church. In Latin countries of Europe and South America, the customary mode of saluting a priest is by kissing the palms of his hands.

With these hands is poured the water of baptism over the heads of infants, without which there is no possibility of salvation at all. These hands are likewise the instruments which will apply the oil of last anointing to the sin-stained senses of dying bodies, an action which is believed to take effect on the soul even after consciousness has fled. The motions of these hands raised in blessing over material objects, chase out the power of evil which is held to be inherent in all matter, after which such objects become sacred and holy things. To employ such objects—medals, scapulars, rosary beads etc.—thereafter for other than spiritual uses is considered desecration. It is by these hands that the devil is exorcized from infants after they are born.

But Roman Catholic priests no longer claim to possess in their hands the power of healing sickness and disease, although it was definitely said by Christ:

"They shall lay their hands on the sick and they shall be healed." Relics of saints from Italy are now applied instead to the bodies of the believing faithful in the hope that they will be cured of their infirmities.

The intricacies of theology, philosophy and the art of preaching count much less in the work of a priest than his anointed hands. A young man may receive ordination to the Roman Catholic priesthood who is intellectually deficient, but not so one who is lacking one joint of either thumb or two joints of an index finger. Personal sanctity is of lesser importance than the left eye, called "the canonical eye," the lack of which constitutes an impediment to ordination, since it would render difficult the reading of the prayers from the mass book which is placed at his left side on the altar. As regards the productive efficiency of the works he performs with his hands, the personal beliefs or morals of a priest do not matter at all, as long as he performs the operations correctly and has the intention of doing what the Church has instructed him to do. It is a necessary fundamental rule of Roman Catholic soteriology that the efficacy of the manipulations of a priest's hands is no way impaired by unbelief or immoral conduct of the priest in his own private life.

Unless he has specially qualified for a teaching position, the young priest beginning his ministry has a very hazy knowledge of what the theology that was taught him in the seminary is all about. A small book called a *ritual* gives him detailed instructions of the manner in which he must perform the various actions deemed essential for the valid administration of the sacraments and other ceremonial acts. The "Church" is his covering and final argument in every doctrinal difficulty presented to him. "The Church," he will answer, "has so decreed it, so you must obey or be damned." The law of the Church and his tabloid ritual-book constitute his entire equipment. His usefulness as a priest is limited to what his hands are endowed to accomplish.

A priest's help to the dying (which many Protestant ministers in America seem to envy) is not due to any personal contact from himself, but to the psychological comfort induced in the dying person by the contact of the act of oil applied by the priest to his lips, nose, hands, feet and other parts of his body. His preaching is mostly about brick and mortar for buildings, and the necessary dollars to cover payment of mortgages, along with frequent appeals to increase attendance at devotions and novenas to the Little Flower, Saint Anthony or Saint Anne.

But the priest cannot be altogether blamed for this. His economic support, his dignity, and his position as mediator between the people and God have been made dependent upon the belief of the people in the magic of external objects—shrines, blest candles, medals, beads, relics and such like. Were he to exert himself to prepare inspiring sermons to raise the people's minds to grasp the true teachings of Jesus Christ, of what use then would it be for him to exhort the people to drop their dimes and dollars into church boxes to light little colored lamps before magical shrines of the Sacred Heart and the Little Flower? Were he to take the trouble to explain the real meaning and message of Calvary, how then could he de-

mand a price for the favor of celebrating the sacrifice
of the mass for those who can afford to pay more than
others for it? If he were to preach the self-develop-
ment of supernatural power and spiritual insight,
how could he then command unquestioned submission
to a pope in Rome as the sole medium of all things
spiritual?

If Roman Catholic priests were to extol the vir-
tues of true education and intellectual progress, how
could they honestly clamor Sunday after Sunday for
the dollars of their poor parishioners to build bigger
and better parochial schools? For in these Catholic
schools education must be in strict accord with the
Church's dogmatic teaching, which consists in stuff-
ing the child's mind with mere one-sided knowledge—
the doctored metaphysics that are essential to protect
the authoritarian system of the Catholic Church. The
first duty of a Roman Catholic priest is to keep his
people in 'simplicity of faith.' In order to do so he is
obliged to leave them in ignorance of facts.

Often the priest himself is confused about many
things that he is obliged to preach to the people. One
of these is the power he is supposed to have to forgive
sins in confession. Does or does not the act of absolution which he pronounces over sinners in the confession box take away their sins? No priest can give a
clear, definite answer to this question. He was taught
that he has the power of forgiving sins, which was
transmitted to him by the authority of the Church in
Rome. But he has no clear understanding of the extent and limitations of this supposed power. The people who come to him for forgiveness, on the other

hand, have no doubt about their belief that pardon for their sins depends entirely on the will and judgment of the absolving priest. But this is not strictly true. For, in theory at least, Roman Catholic theologians admit that sins can, in some cases, be forgiven without absolution of a priest.

The whole difficulty, of course, centers around the absurdity that sins can be forgiven week after week in the same way as you pay off your debts to your grocer, after which you can begin again to contract further debts. The Jesuit theologians have made it more difficult still by distinguishing between different kinds of contrition or sorrow for sin. One kind they call 'perfect' contrition, the other 'imperfect' contrition, for which they have coined a special word *attrition*. A person who has only this attrition for his sins is said to be sorry for them, not because his sins have offended God, but because he is afraid he will go to hell unless he obtains forgiveness of them from the priest.

It can easily be seen that this is fear, not sorrow or true repentance. For it means that if there were no hell, such a person would not be sorry at all for having sinned, and would keep on sinning all the time with impunity. But according to Roman Catholic teaching, if a person with this feeling of mere attrition for his sins confesses them to a priest, then his sins are washed away as soon as the priest makes the sign of the cross over the sinner's head and pronounces the prescribed formula of absolution. But not all together. Immediate danger of going to hell only is removed, but there remains an unknown amount of guilt which must be expiated for, either in this life by penances, or in the next life by burning in purgatory.

It is taught that, in rare instances, sins can be forgiven without the absolution of a priest. There are two conditions attached to this supposition: if the person is dying and a priest is not available, and if the sinner can work up 'perfect' contrition. Furthermore, if such a person recovers he is obliged to go and confess his sins, already pardoned, to a priest as soon as he can find one. If not, then in some mysterious way that no one can explain, his sins come back. In fact, if he fails to do so, another sin is added, namely, one of grave disobedience to the law of the Church.

It is entirely unscriptural that 'attrition' is sufficient to obtain forgiveness of sins. In the Christian dispensation, "the blood of Jesus Christ alone cleanses from all sin." This is obtained by true repentance, *metanoia,* a change of heart, and is a complete and perfect pardon. Confessing to a priest to obtain his forgiveness is the pagan, pre-Christian way. But it serves to enhance the power of the priest to whom the people trust for pardon of their sins before they die.

This teaching explains the anxiety of Roman Catholics to make sure they will have the priest when they come to die, and it is for this reason that we see pictures in newspapers of priests rushing dramatically into burning buildings, or to the scene of automobile smash-ups, to reach the burned and mangled bodies of the victims before they expire. The people firmly believe that the priest alone has the power to give them a ticket to heaven, even though it leads through the flames of an excruciating purgatory. To know that "he had the priest" at the end, relieves the anxiety of many a Catholic mother's heart about the salvation of a wayward son, even if he dies in the electric chair.

Parents and friends of those killed in automobile wrecks and airplane crashes are consoled to hear that a priest was in the locality, even some distance away. I once knew a Catholic mother whose son was killed in a plane crash, and who was broken-hearted at first because there was no priest present to absolve him. But her sorrow disappeared afterward when a priest wrote to tell her that he had seen the accident from a passing train and had made the sign of absolution in the air to forgive the sins of those in the plane.

In practice, however, it is made the rule that only by the absolution of a priest can a sinner be pardoned from his sins and saved from eternal punishment in hell. Priests make it known that generally speaking it is almost impossible to work up 'perfect' contrition for sin, for perfect sorrow is equal to perfect love of God, something that only heroic saints can have. In this way, the obligation to come to confession is stressed. To clinch the argument, they will quote verse 22 of the 20th chapter of the Gospel of *John* (Catholic version): *"Whose sins you shall forgive they are forgiven them, and whose sins you shall retain they are retained."*

This verse of Scripture, they tell their people, makes it plain that only priests of the Roman Catholic Church have the power to forgive and to refuse to forgive sins. They do not explain that Jesus Christ said this to both apostles and disciples, among whom were some women. Neither do they explain the context, in which Christ mentioned two distinct 'missions,' one, His mission from the Father—which was to die upon the cross to forgive the sins of the world, and which only He could do—and the other, the commission to his apostles and disciples to go forth and preach the Gospel message that sins have been remitted by His finished work on Calvary. Protestant ministers carry out this commission to remit sins, but in the correct sense that they declare that sins are forgiven, and that sinners are saved, "to the uttermost," by this redeeming work of Jesus Christ. For who can forgive sins but God alone?

This matter of the forgiveness of sins has been made so confusing in Catholic Church teaching that the bewildered young priest soon ceases to argue how it is done. He takes it for granted that all he has to do is to make the sign of the cross and pronounce the prescribed formula over the heads of the thousands of sinners who kneel down before him in the confession box. Some priests become very careless about it and ask no questions of their penitents. Others require that every detail of sins confessed must be explained to them, and that it depends upon the judgment of the priest whether or not the sinner can be pardoned. They are especially severe on women who try to conceal the details of their marital relations with their husbands in the matter of birth control.

The word 'confession' and 'going to confession' are ill-advised and no substitute for true repentance for sin. The former implies merely the telling of sins and the number of times committed to a priest in order to get his absolution. It is not surprising that credulous Catholic people are led to believe that this is all that is required. It has been well proved that the Catholic practice of confession is no deterrent against crime. This can be seen from examination of the crime records of any large city in the United States. In New York State, for example, where Roman Catholics number only about 26 per cent of the total population, a disproportionate number of crimes are committed by Roman Catholics who are trained from childhood to the forced practice of sacramental confession[1] Even Roman Catholic statisticians admit the fact that the Roman Catholic populations of the jails and penitentiaries in nearly all States far exceed the proportion of Roman Catholics in the general population. In some States Catholic criminals outnumber non-Catholics by as much as four to one.[2] Roman Catholics comprise only about 16 per cent of the total population of the United States.

To the average Roman Catholic priest, the absolving of sinners in confession becomes a very routine matter, a tiresome sawing of the sign of the cross in the air over the heads of his confessing parishioners, accompanied by the mechanical repetition of the Latin

---

[1] cf. *Annual Reports of the Commissioner of Correction* of the State of New York, for the years 1940 to 1946, where it is shown that a consistent 50 per cent of criminals committed to New York's two largest prisons, Sing Sing and Dannemora, year after year, are Roman Catholics.

[2] cf. *Crime and Religion,* by Father Leo Kalmer, O. F. M., preface by the Very Rev. Francis J. Haas, Ph. D. Franciscan Herald Press, Chicago, 1936; a statistical survey of Catholics in jails compiled by Roman Catholic chaplains of State and Federal prisons in the U. S. See also, *Religious Education and Crime,* by L. H. Lehmann, pamphlet, Agora Publishing Co., New York.

words of absolution. The whole process is in no way spiritually directive and has little psychological value.

An action of the priest's hands of even greater importance is the pouring of the water of baptism over the heads of infants. If this action is not properly performed the infant will be cast out of the sight of God for all eternity—even if he grows up and professes full faith in Jesus Christ. No other sacrament of the Catholic Church is of any avail to a person who was not properly baptized in the beginning. The three essential words which the priest must be sure to say while pouring the water are: *Ego te baptizo.* Woe to the child if the priest, by inadvertence or a slip of the tongue, should say the formula for confession, *Ego te absolvo,* which is so much alike and which he repeats many thousands of times. Should this mistake occur, the entire act of baptism would be invalidated, and the child would be a Christian in name only. The unconscious antics of the baby, the sudden contact of cold water on its head, the embarrassing, but perfectly natural accidents that happen to new-born babies at unexpected moments, may conspire to unsteady the hand of the priest while pouring the water or divert his mind from the correct word formula. This pouring of the water of baptism is made so essential for the attainment of heaven, that exact instructions and suitable instruments are provided to perform this action upon a fetus still in its mother's womb, if it appears likely that it may die before issue.

An infant, because born of natural intercourse, is regarded by the Roman Catholic theologians as possessed by the devil after it comes from its mother's

womb.   The priest's first task, therefore, is to cast
out this unclean spirit from the child before baptism.
To this end he uses the most powerful exorcisms accompanied by the sprinkling of holy water and repeated signs of the cross.   He puts salt (previously
exorcized) into the infant's mouth, wets the infant's
lips, ears and nostrils with spittle from his own
mouth, rubs oil on its chest and back.   Directly ad-
dressing the devil which is believed to be in the child,
the priest commands him as follows: "Depart, thou
accursed devil (*maledicte diabole*) from this servant
of God."

Rosary beads, scapulars, medals, chalices and
mass vestments must likewise be cleansed from the
evil which is supposed to be inherent in them as natural and material objects.   After being thus exorcized
they are looked upon as holy objects to be handled with
reverence and used exclusively for acts of worship.
It is a sin for a layman to touch the chalice used by
the priest at mass. It thus comes about that Catholics
believe that such objects, after being blessed by a
priest, possess a magical charm and are able to ward
off the power of the devil and to protect from accidents
their person and property. Blest medals of Saint Christopher are pinned to automobiles (even by some Protestants) in the belief that by so doing cars and their
occupants will be protected from wrecks.   But insurance companies allow no rebate on insurance
premiums for cars that carry one of these blest medals
of Saint Christopher.

Priests personally have little faith in relics of the
saints, medals, beads, scapulars and statues, even

though it is part of their work to exorcize the evil from them and to recommend their use to the pious faithful. Priests who have been to Rome for any length of time lose reverence for such things because of the shameless traffic carried on there in bits of bones and all kinds of pious objects. Rome is a vast graveyard of skulls and bones of supposed saints. In some churches the lamps and ornamentations around the walls are fashioned from bones of departed holy people. In Rome are two heads of Saint Paul, a slipper of Saint Joseph, the girdle of the Virgin Mary, and what is said to be milk from her breasts.

All this ritualistic maneuvering has been invented by the Roman theologians to fit in with their basic teaching that salvation can only be gained by "the works that are worked" by a priest. The grace of salvation is taught as something that can be 'poured' into people's souls through the specially devised channels of the seven sacraments. These in turn are supposed to act as conduits from the great reservoir of grace over which the pope in Rome has sole monopoly. This engineering of external unrealities, to act with magical force to produce a spiritual effect, runs through the entire system of Roman Catholic theology. The works of a priest's hands must be accepted both as a matter of belief as well as of organization and practice.

But of such is not the power of the kingdom of heaven.

CHAPTER NINETEEN

ROME'S SALVATION BY LAW

EVERYTHING in the well-geared mechanism of the Roman Catholic Church is regulated by a complex system of law. The technicalities of this legislative code are applied with exactitude to every thought, word, act and omission of its members—from what, when and how much one may eat and drink, to the intimate details of the manner and frequency of sexual intercourse between husband and wives.

This system of legislation is not a mere abstract, theoretical or speculative blueprint. Disobedience of its requirements exposes one to the risk of eternal damnation. For in the Roman Catholic Church a man's relation to God and his chances of eternal salvation are determined, not by the quality or measure of his spiritual growth, but by jurisprudence.

This framework of law, by which men are judged worthy of heaven or condemned to hell, was taken over in its entirety from the law and penal system of pagan Rome. The Catholic Church's own existence by universal succession, its pardons and indulgences, its *privilegia*, the protection of its property rights by the establishment of impersonal corporations known as "moral persons," all are part of the law system of imperial Rome. Its chief aim is the conservation and advancement of the corporative structure of the Roman papacy. In his valuable treatise, *Christian*

Thought to the Reformation, Professor Work explains the set-up as follows:[1]

"In its conception, the individual, *as individual,* has no place. His salvation is conditioned from first to last by his belonging to a *corporation,* in whose principles and functions he shares (according to certain conditions laid down) and by whose sacramental life (also according to certain conditions) his soul is nourished. Through this corporation alone is he brought into touch with his Saviour; outside this corporation his soul is lost."

By this incorporation, the millions of individual consciences of its obedient members are merged into the corporate conscience residing in the supreme pontifex, the pope, in Rome. Upon his absolute and unquestionable rulings depends the eternal salvation of all. Furthermore, whether they like it or not, the salvation of all mankind is made to depend upon the will of this Roman pontifex and the laws he makes. Not only baptized Roman Catholics, but all Christians are counted as members of this mammoth Roman corporation. It is claimed that they, too, could be obliged, under penalty of eternal damnation, to attend mass every Sunday and to abstain from eating more than two ounces of meat on Fridays. Few Protestants know that it is only since the promulgation of the *Ne Temere* decree of Pope Pius X in 1908, that their marriages, although performed by their own ministers, have been counted as valid by the Roman Catholic Church.

---

[1] In *Ency. of Religion,* vol. XI, p. 706.

This bold claim of ·the Roman Catholic Church
to be the universal law maker for all Christians is
fundamental to the whole structure of Roman Church
law. It is asserted that this absolute and universal
power has been transmitted through the apostle Peter
to all the popes of Rome from Christ. This claim was
made irrevocable by the bull *Unam Sanctam* of Pope
Boniface VIII in 1302, which decreed that "every
creature," civil and ecclesiatical, is dependent for salvation upon the laws and regulations issued by the
Roman papacy. In 1870, the decree of Pope Pius IX
in the Vatican Council, which defined as a dogma of
faith the absolute supremacy and the personal infallibility of all the popes of Rome before and after him,
confirmed and broadened the claim of Boniface VIII,
making it, now and for all time, an unalterable truth
in the galaxy of fixed Roman dogmas.

The hard, rigorous lines of the Roman legal
structure of this papal corporation are carried over
and applied to its conception·of the spiritual life. This
spiritual structure is made strangely anatomical. It
has its directing head and automatically responsive
members. Of utmost importance are its indispensable
veins—the seven sacraments—which act as channels
through which the life stream of grace can alone flow
into the souls of all men. The wafer of holy communion has recently been made the necessary sustaining
food as well as the remedial and preventive medicine
for all its members. The confessional is its exhaust—
the excretionary organ for the release of accumulated
waste and injurious matter—the purifying process
of the body corporate. The intricate network of cen-

turies of theological casuistry is its protective skin
shielding it against outside inimical and heretical
forces.

This papal corporation also has its spiritual
treasury—a vast banking center—which holds the
huge reserves of grace. These are the accumulation
of the superabundant gains, not only of Christ's redemptive work, but also of the excess profits earned
by what are called the works of 'supererogation' of the
Virgin Mary and the saints. The key to this treasure
is in the sole keeping of the pope. He alone can dispense at will of the stored grace through many channels, some of which, like the seven sacraments, are set
for all time, others for special occasions, such as, for
instance, when he proclaims a special jubilee and
grants indulgences and pardons by drawing upon the
extensive credit balance of these reserves.

Modern methods of advertising and propaganda,
to overcome spiritual sales resistance, were known and
practiced by this Roman Catholic world-corporation
long before American business copied and put them
into use in our commercial world today. I do not think
that any commercial business agent has been able to
improve upon the efficiency of the propaganda methods of the Roman Catholic Church. The very word
'propaganda' was originally coined by the Roman
Catholic Church for the special purpose of publicizing
its doctrines and claims. The word has been plagia-
rized and made into a science today by business men
and politicians.

As used by business and politics today, Roman
Catholic propaganda has always had its main appeal

to the human fear-complex. History proves how this
has been cleverly played upon by the propagandists
of the Roman Catholic Church during the Middle
Ages. Business and politics play upon the fear of
earthly discomforts—the fear of pyorrhea for all at
forty unless you use a certain kind of toothpaste; of
a double chin or throat injury, which only can be a-
voided by smoking a certain brand of cigarettes; of
the billions of disease-carrying germs that infect
every breath of you and your neighbor; of the super-
iority of the Joneses because they own a bigger and
better automobile than yours. To add to these fears
created in the mind by radio and sales talk, glaring
picturizations of them are made to catch your eye
wherever you go. Even the most skeptical in time become conscious of the need of the protection offered
by the use of the articles so advertised.

   These advertising methods are copies of the more
effective play upon the fear-complex of spiritual ruin
originated by the propagandists of the Roman Catholic Church many centuries ago. Men fear most what
they cannot see, especially when it concerns eternal
life in heaven or hell after death. There is no sacrifice
or suffering that believers in God and the hereafter
will not make if convinced that it is necessary in order
to obtain happiness beyond the grave.

   It was easy for the Catholic Church all through
the centuries to create the consciousness in its members of the absolute need of corporate protection from
the danger of eternal damnation. It used glaringly
colored pictures of an eternal flaming hell and the
cruel pitchforks of grinning devils to stress the need

of the saving grace which only a priest of the Catholic
Church can obtain for a soul before its fearful journey
through the portals of death. These same pictures may
be seen in the homes and churches of Roman Catholics
today. Souls of departed loved ones are pictured in the
searing flames of purgatory, their arms upraised
beseeching from those on earth the prayers and masses
which can alone soothe them in their torment.
This grace is painted in these pictures as being poured
upon these burning souls by the merciful hands of the
Virgin Mary. The quantity thus doled out is believed
to be limited by the number of masses which priests
are paid to say for these suffering souls. The golden
gates giving entrance to eternal bliss in heaven are
pictured as opening only to the magic touch of the
hands of Roman Catholic priests.

The executives of this papal corporation are the
bishops and priests. They alone have the power of re-
mitting sins and dispensing grace. But this power
they in turn can receive only from the supreme pontiff
in Rome. Bishops are appointed and receive their spiritual powers directly from the pope in Rome. All their
credentials permitting them to exercise these powers
are worded in the preamble as follows: *"By favor of
the Apostolic Roman See . . . "* Since this is granted
only as a matter of favor, the pope can withdraw this
power from bishops and priests at will.

The Catholic people also live in constant fear that
the grace of spiritual benefits may be taken from them
at any time. If a congregation of lay Catholics should
object even to the disposal of a piece of Church property, or the appointment of a pastor, the threat of the

denial of the grace of salvation will immediately follow. If a priest should refuse to obey an order of his
bishop to remove himself to another parish, the power
of transmitting the grace of salvation to his people
and of absolving them from their sins is promptly cut
off from him. For this grace of salvation is made to
flow from the pope through the fingers of the priest to
the souls of his congregation. It can be cut off as
promptly and efficiently as the electric current from
your home if you fail to pay your bill to the utility
company.

The foundation of the Roman Catholic Church is
rooted in its claim to be a perfect corporate entity,
whose charter was written in heaven by Almighty God
and delivered on earth to the popes of Rome by Jesus
Christ. It is further claimed that this charter makes
the Roman papacy independent of and superior to all
human corporations and institutions. This claim was
made to function among the nations of Europe by the
"theory of the two powers," of the two and only two
"perfect societies" that ever can exist—the Roman
Catholic Church and the State, represented by the Pope
and Emperor; two dictators, one in the Church and
one in the State. The two are held to be independent
only in theory, however. In practice the State must
bow to the superior power of the Church.

This corporate law system through which the
Roman Catholic Church pretends to be able to dispense and withhold the grace of salvation is a direct
denial of the whole spirit of Christ's teaching. It is
rooted in the error that the spiritual kingship of
Christ is a mere second edition of Caesarism flavored

with an external sacramental process. It continues to make law the universal schoolmaster and contradicts St. Paul who says (*Gal.*3: 24-26): "But before faith came, we were kept under the law, shut up unto the faith which should afterwards be revealed. *Wherefore the law was our schoolmaster to bring us unto Christ* that we might be justified by faith. *But after that faith is come, we are no longer under a schoolmaster. For ye are all children of God in Christ Jesus.*"

Thomas Jefferson, father of American democracy, copied St. Paul when he declared: "The care of every man's soul belongs to himself. No man has the power to let another prescribe his faith . . . History, I believe, furnishes no example of a priest-ridden people maintaining a free civil government."

From this contradiction of true Christian teaching in the Roman Catholic Church flow all the other contradictions and spiritual poverty so evident in every phase of its beliefs and practices. The Bible at once became a danger to its over-weighted law structure and had to be denied to the people. On the other hand, the Bible had to be preserved as a mere reference book for the theologians and priests to sustain the power of the priesthood by plausible, elastic interpretation of certain texts. But as far as the people are concerned, the existence of God's autobiography is best forgotten.

Roman Catholic people never stop to think that Jesus Christ completely ignored the High Priest and the seventy members of the Sanhedrin of the Jewish Church. He always spoke directly to the people along the country roads, in the fields, by the lake shore and in the public market place. Only on great festival days did He enter the synagogue, and then only because on such occasions He had access to a larger crowd of people. Law or metaphysics never entered into His discourses, nor did the political intrigues of kings and statesmen in the least way ever influence His teaching of the message of the kingdom of heaven and His new way of salvation. Even when these people came and tried by force to make him king, "he fled away into the mountains alone."

The pope of Rome, on the other hand, who claims to substitute for the same Jesus Christ on earth, insists on being a king, the king of kings. When the tiara, or triple crown, is placed upon his head at his coronation ceremony, the ritual prescribes the following declaration: "*Receive the tiara adorned with three crowns, and know that thou art the Father of Princes and Kings, Ruler of the World, and Vicar of our Saviour Jesus Christ.*"[2] Thus this so-called 'vicar of Jesus Christ' accepts the position of ruler of the world which the devil offered to Christ, but which Christ spurned with the command to Satan: "Get thee hence!"

The hierarchy of honors, distinctions and titles among the clergy of the Roman Catholic Church is the natural consequence of the sky-high position taken by its supreme ruler. The longer the list of grades and shades of distinctions ascending and descending the hierarchical ladder, the nearer the highest rung

---

[2] Quoted from the official *National Catholic Almanac* for 1942, p. 171.

on which the pope sits approaches the misty skyline separating earth from heaven.

Jesus Christ made Himself the lowliest of men. But by this He did not mean that Christianity must be identified with poverty and misery. He meant it as an example that the new order of relationship that He established among men and between men and God was to be one of universal brotherhood and divine sonship. He made it clear that this new order would be destroyed by the assumption of prerogatives by any one member of the Kingdom, even by the one who is elected to preside over the others. This is carried out to the letter in our American republican form of government whose chief executive (of the most powerful and wealthiest country of all history) is called simply, "Mr. President."

For it can easily be seen that the moment even one such prerogative or title is given to any one individual, by which he is raised one step above his fellows, others directly below him must be given a lower grade of honor or title, in order to make his foothold secure and to enhance the pre-eminence thus accorded to him. This pre-eminence of superiors ascends in relation to the descent of inferiors, until top and bottom respectively reach zenith and nadir. He on top is thus pushed up until he becomes lost, from the neck up, in the clouds of heaven. Those at the bottom are pushed down until their feet rest on the very floor of hell. Victims for this hell must be found the moment a triple-crowned pope on his throne begins to make his laws and launch his anathemas.

In such a religious system the need at once arises for law and metaphysics, even though these are divorced from ethics and human needs. Salvation for all, except a favored few, is made dependent upon the laws fashioned by the one at the top of the ladder. The pope himself is able to shake hands with the Almighty in the clouds of heaven, not because of any individual merit or sanctity on his part, but by virtue of the old Roman law of universal succession. By the same law code of ancient Rome, disobedient outcasts are thrown upon the pitchforks of the devil in hell.

The pope is called "His Holiness" (*Sua Santità di Nostro Signore*—"The Sanctity of our Lord"), even though he should be the greatest villain on earth. Cardinals are called "Eminent Princes;" bishops are "Your Lordships;" monsignors "Most Illustrious;" priests "Very Reverend" or just mere "Reverend." Kings and princes obedient to the pope are placed in special compartments, such as "The Supreme Order of Christ;" "His Most Catholic Majesty." Rich laymen are given titles of "Marquis" "Knights" and "Commanders." The great mass of the people go unnamed, and are referred to as "the simple faithful," the servitors. Finally, as if made to bear the whole weight of this towering structure of titles, honors and distinctions, the "heretics" are crushed underneath it all and branded as *anathema*.

Each ascending grade in the Roman Catholic hierarchy has its own exclusive ritualistic function to perform; also its own distinctive shade of dress to wear.

These are shared by all above that grade, but denied to all beneath. The pope can wear all the vestments of all the other grades beneath him, plus those that he alone can wear: his triple crown, his cloak trimmed in ermine, and white cassock. Only he may drink from the mass chalice through a golden tube and seated on his throne. All others drink from the chalice direct and standing at the altar. Only the pope may be carried aloft on men's shoulders. Only he may have his toe kissed, and only before him are carried the oriental ostrich plumes, called the *flabellae*.

Even the power of forgiving the sins of the people is meted out according to grade. A simple parish priest may only absolve certain classes of sins. A bishop is limited in forgiving sins only by special reservations made by the Grand Penitentiary in Rome, and by the power of the pope to forgive a choice selection of sins. The pope alone can forgive every kind and degree of sin committed by all classes of people. A bishop, at certain times, can grant an indulgence up to three hundred days. There seems to be no limit to the amount and quantity of indulgences that the pope, by his own power, can grant at any time.

Even cardinals are not of equal grade. Some are cardinal deacons; others cardinal priests; others cardinal bishops and archbishops. Bishops are also graded, and are distinguished by the number of tassels hanging from their hats. Monsignors are allowed an extra lighted candle at mass. For a bishop two extra tapers are lighted, and for all those above bishops in dignity as many tapers are permitted as

occasion demands.   Monsignors are facetiously called
'mule bishops' by the lower clergy, because they cannot, like fully consecrated bishops, generate priests.
They may, however, wear purple on their street dress
and some are allowed to wear the miter and vestments
of a bishop when saying mass on special occasions.

Such elaborate ritual is foreign to Christian worship and destructive of true Christian teaching.   It
lowers faith to mere credulity and superstition.   It
endows priests with a fictitious character of dignity
and mysterious awe.   The injunctions of Jesus Christ
are opposed to such priestly dignity. Much of it grows
out of the mystifying mannerisms of priests, the
mumble-jumble of the unknown tongue they use at
the altar, the dimly burning tapers, the whiff of the
incense and flowers associated with their every action
on the altar.   These may be all right in a theater, but
are out of place in a Christian church.

This legal and ritualistic spirit of Roman Catholicism is not the spirit of Christ.   It is a pagan spirit
dogmatized into Christianity to suit the ends of Roman
Catholic power.   The true spirit of Christ does not
lend itself to law and ritual, but rather is destructive
of them, since by means of them men are enslaved, not
made free.   Christ's formula for freedom is knowledge of the truth.

CHAPTER TWENTY-ONE

THE TRUE PRIESTHOOD OF CHRIST

N O SECRET is made of the unscriptural teaching about priests in the Roman Catholic Church. It is boldly proclaimed on every possible occasion that Roman Catholic priests are mediators between God and man and that they are endowed with the power of offering up daily a sacrifice of propitiation for the sins of men.

A typical example of this was had at the funeral service for Msgr. William T. Conklin at St. Saviour's Church, in Brooklyn, N. Y. on November 3, 1942. In the funeral oration over the dead priest, Monsignor H. Casey, the preacher declared, according to the Brooklyn *Tablet* of the following November 6: "*A priest is called by God, and rightly so, to act as a mediator between God and man, and to offer a sacrifice of propitiation for the sins of men.*"

Here we have an example of how Roman Catholic teaching has "turned the truth of God into a lie." Yet, among the hundreds of bishops, monsignors, priests and nuns who were present on that occasion, not one raised a voice in protest against this flagrant contradiction of the true Christian teaching about salvation. No interpreter or 'infallible' pope is needed to expound the Scripture teaching on this point, and to show at once how pagan is this claim that a mere man can be a mediator between God and man and is able

to offer up sacrifice for the sins of men.   The epistle
to the *Hebrews* (10: 14) makes it crystal clear that:

*"By one offering He hath perfected for ever them that
are sanctified."*   And again (*Heb.* 10: 12) : *"But this
man (Christ) after he had offered one sacrifice for
sins for ever, sat down on the right hand of God."*
And again (10:10) ; *"By the which we are sanctified
through the offering of the body of Jesus Christ once
for all."*

As a converted priest, I now rejoice in belonging
to the body of believers who in the New Testament
are called, by Saint Peter himself, "an holy priesthood" (1 *Pet.* 2: 5).   In the true Church of God in
the Christian dispensation all believers are priests.
There is now no separate class specially called priests
who are nearer to God than are other believers.   In
Israel there was a separate class called priests, but
not in Christian Churches.   Ministers as such, in the
New Testament writings, are never called priests.

There is no single service of God's worship that
any Christian is incompetent to perform.   The family
principle is that which dominates the priesthood of
the true Christian Church.   Whosoever is a member
of the family of faith is a priest, be he minister or layman.   As members of this household of the faith we
may have different appointments of service which are
bestowed on each.   But whatever our station, as believers in Christ, we are all priests.

This is the day for spiritual sacrifices, "a living
sacrifice, holy, acceptable unto God, which is our rea-

sonable service." The world is weary of sacerdotalism and has no more use for ecclesiasticism. Every true believer must realize anew the great privilege that is his as a priest of the Most High God and grasp the tremendous opportunity to serve according to his divinely bestowed gift. We are "a chosen generation," Saint Peter again tells us, "a royal priesthood, a holy nation, a peculiar people; that we should show forth the praises of him who called us out of darkness into his marvelous light."

Not only are we priests, but also kings—a "royal" priesthood, Saint Peter tells us. This revolutionary doctrine was meant to turn the world upside down (*Acts* 17: 6). This is the teaching that ushered in the 'new order' of the Christian dispensation. Peter would have been untrue to his Master had he taught that one man could be an autocrat over others in spiritual matters. Peter's teaching is that each one is his own priest and his own king. This is democracy with a vengeance! It follows that since each one is his own priest, he must also possess within himself the highest governing power and, as in our American democracy, merely delegates this power, by election and for a stated time, to those whom he chooses to represent him in the public forum.

I do not think that the real implications of this new teaching of the Christian dispensation are sufficiently understood by most people. If they fully understood its meaning and acted upon it, it would seem to be impossible for them to allow such flagrant perversion of it to exist among them.

We are again fully assured of our royal status in Christ by Saint John in *Rev.* 1: 5, 6: *"Unto him that loved us and washed us from our sins in his own blood, and hath made us kings and priests unto God and his Father; to him be glory and dominion for ever and ever, Amen."*

THE CONVERSION OF MARTIN LUTHER

ERASMUS, the scholarly, humanist contemporary of Luther, once shrewdly said of him: *"Luther committed two unpardonable sins. He attacked the power of the pope and the bellies of the monks."* Erasmus was also a rebellious priest but, unlike Luther, gained fame and retained the good will of the ecclesiastical authorities by attacking the abuses of the Church solely on the intellectual level. Himself a priest and the son of a priest, Erasmus kept on such good terms with the pope that he even obtained release from the law of celibacy. Unlike Luther he seems to have experienced no spiritual conversion. By his clever ridicule he discredited the inanities of the corrupt system of Catholic Church learning known as Scholasticism, but he played safe and kept well out of the way of the anathemas and heresy-hunting agents of the pope.

The lasting work of reform accomplished by Luther was due to the fact that he acted from personal conviction as a result of his own spiritual conversion. He kindled a fire of the spirit which is not easy to extinguish. Erasmus' adventure was intellectual. Luther's was spiritual and therefore involved greater risks but resulted in tremendous blessings for humanity. Of Erasmus Luther wrote to Spalatin in March 1517: *"I must confess that his sharp and undiminished attack upon the ignorance of the priests*

*and monks pleases me.   But I fear that he does not
promote the cause of Christ and God's grace sufficiently.   For him human considerations have an absolute preponderance over divine. . . . No one is truly
wise in the Christian sense simply because he knows
Greek and Hebrew.*"

The splendid story of young Luther, *Road to
Reformation,** by Heinrich Boehmer, recently translated and published in English, shows how similar
were the experiences of the great Protestant reformer
to those of priests today who are also converted to
Evangelical Christianity.   Chapter ten of Boehmer's
work appeals most to me.   For it depicts Luther's
first steps toward the realization of salvation by grace
and of the uselessness of the ritualistic practices and
theology of Roman Catholicism.   What Luther went
through to arrive at this, is similar to what I and
every other converted priest experienced.   The process is one of great soul anguish, doubt, hesitation and
even of great temptation to resist the dawning consciousness of the light that God shines upon the soul.
It was the fear of hell, the only escape from which is
made to depend upon adherence to Roman Catholic
beliefs and practices, that drove young Luther into
the priesthood in the Augustinian Order.

As I also argued with myself before I became a
priest, Luther seemed to have convinced himself that
since a priest is empowered to forgive sins and dispense the grace of salvation to others, one of the
surest ways of avoiding hell for himself was to be-

---

* Muhlenberg Press, Phila., Pa.

come a priest. I can well understand the shock he suffered when he realized later, as most priests eventually do, that forgiveness of sins in the Catholic confessional had no effect on him, that he was just the same after confession as before.

It was only when Luther turned to the famous passage in *Romans* 1:16-17, that he began to understand how sins are really forgiven and how different is the Gospel teaching about salvation to that of Roman Catholic theology. For there he saw for the first time how the Gospel is *the very power of God,* because *"therein is the righteousness of God revealed from faith unto faith."* But for Luther this at first was a further cause of doubt and despair. "Thus the Gospel too," he complained, "is only a revelation of the punitive righteousness of God, only a means of further torturing and tormenting men who are already fearfully burdened with original sin and the Ten Commandments."

According to Boehmer (p. 110) this thought actually engendered in Luther a feeling of passionate hatred of this cruel God who always requires love and yet actually makes it impossible for His creatures to love him. It was only after he had carefully examined the context to this passage of Romans that he saw that what is meant is not the *punitive* righteousness of God, but rather the *forgiving* righteousness of God by which His mercy makes us just, as it is written: *justus ex fide vivit.* *"Then it seemed to me,"* Luther declared, *"as if I were born anew and that I had entered into the open gates of paradise. The whole Bible suddenly took on a new aspect for me. I ran through*

*it, as much as I had it in my memory, and gathered
together a great number of similar expressions as
'work of God,' that is, that which God works in us;
'power of God,' that is, the power through which He
makes us powerful; 'wisdom of God,' that is, the
wisdom through which He makes us wise .... As
much as I had heretofore hated the word 'righteousness' of God, so much the more dear and sweet it was
to me now. And so that passage of St. Paul became for
me in very truth the gate to paradise.*"

In my own experience, I remember actually pray-
ing against this light, that God would *not* convince me
that I must take the consequences of it and break
from the priesthood and its associations, from the love
of family and friends. I can well understand now
what Luther meant when he described the effect of his
decision as "*a new insight and a new sense of life.*"
On that same day that the light came to him, Luther
wrote a commentary on Psalm 31, which he entitled:
"*Concerning the means of true repentance, that sins
are remitted, not by any works, but alone by the
mercy of God without any merit.*"

Those whose knowledge of Luther is limited will
be amazed to discover the volume of work he accomplished—his ability to compose and have published
treatise after treatise in such short order. Notable
among these were: *An Open Letter to the Christian
Nobility of the German Nation concerning the Reform of the Christian Estate* (begun June 6, 1521,
and on the press by June 23) ; *A Prelude to the Baby-
lonian Captivity of the Church* (begun August 31 and
off the press by October 6 of the same year) ; *On Mon-*

astic Vows (written between November 21 and December 1, 1521). Within six months after the famous Leipsig Disputation, Luther published sixteen treatises, including three polemics against Eck and Emser. These comprise some fifty of our average printed signatures today. He delivered about two signatures to the printery every week. In addition, he usually preached two or three times, lectured at least two hours, and continued to conduct occasional disputations with his students. He wrote in Latin and German, and once he had begun to write, he usually sent the finished sheets to the neighboring print shops without going over them again. He changed hardly anything in the proofs.

His *Open Letter to the Christian Nobility* pulled the props from under the whole Roman Catholic structure of medieval thought, doctrine, practice and law —especially the pet Roman doctrine of *the two estates, the two laws* and *the two powers of Pope and Emperor.* Every Christian is a priest, he declared; the Christian does not need a human mediator to enter into relationship with God, nor does God need human mediators to communicate with man; every Christian is empowered to proclaim the Word of God; priestly celibacy was to be abolished and congregations have the right to elect their pastors. To be abolished also were: all holy days except Sunday; all Church fairs, pilgrimages, indulgences, chapels and shrines in uninhabited places; masses for the dead; monasteries of mendicant friars were to be closed, and the monks be forbidden to beg, preach and hear confessions; monasteries and foundations should be turned into schools and perpetual vows abolished. He also recommended the communion cup for the laity, as the Hussites had done before him. Of the greatest importance was Luther's insistence on the principle—which has since been made the groundwork of all democratic governments—that *"there are not two estates nor are there two powers in Christendom, for power or force may not be used at all in spiritual affairs.* Power to compel (*potestas coactiva*) belongs solely to the secular government, and it is to be applied only in temporal affairs."* For herein is the whole basis of Protestantism's great principle of *religious freedom,* and the outright denial of any power in the Church of Rome to persecute and kill heretics—a claim which the Roman Catholic Church outrageously clings to even in this twentieth century.

So complete was Luther's amazing reform that nothing seemed to remain of the whole complex of ideas which had formed the basis of the social, political, and legal thought of the Western world as controlled by the papacy from Rome for nearly a thousand years.

Yet Luther was no *innovator,* but rather a *renovator.* His was a plain *reassertion* of the Gospel truth that was hidden for so long from the people. He founded no new religion, was not a fanatic, a starry-eyed mystic, nor did he ever claim to have had visions or special revelations from God to start anything new. He was no miracle-worker, nor did he need signs and wonders, as are generally attributed to Rome's saints, to bring about his reassertion of the true Gospel teaching and the magnificent results that followed automatically for the nations of Europe that accepted his reforms.

Was Luther without fault? Far from it. If I may dare to agree with Boehmer, I, too, would accuse Luther of making the mistake of trying to pour the new wine of the reasserted Gospel into some of the old bottles of Roman ecclesiasticism. Protestantism generally has suffered from this defect ever since, and in some instances has lost ground in our day, is even inclined to an envious and slavish imitation of Roman Catholicism in many things. It is safe to say that, if this new wine of the Gospel had been allowed to flow full and free to the people in the market-place, the "revolt of the masses," the violent upheaval that threatens all Christendom today, might have been avoided. I would say that the excesses of Bolshevistic communism can be traced to the fact that the masses of the common people were allowed merely to taste— and that too belatedly—the new wine of the freedom of the Gospel. In Roman Catholic countries especially —also in Eastern Orthodox countries such as Russia —that taste was obtained from the narrow bottles of corrupt ecclesiasticism.

There remains for us in this century of wildly drifting humanity the task of carrying to completeness the work of spiritual revival started by Martin Luther.

WHAT WOULD CHRIST SAY TODAY?

I HAVE OFTEN tried to imagine what Jesus Christ would say today to the Roman Catholic Church if he were to appear again on earth. In the book of Revelation he gave messages to John for the seven Churches, but the Church of Rome was not amongst them.

He would, of course, be asked to broadcast over the radio, on a world-wide hook-up. But before being allowed to do so, he would have to consult with a committee of the Conference of Christians and Jews. They would inform him of their censorship rules: 1) never to "attack" any religion; 2) never to "condemn" anyone; 3) never to use strong language or say too much about "hell." He would be told that the Washington censorship bureau had recently clamped down on any kind of criticism that would arouse religious conflicts; and, in general, to pretend that there is really very litle difference among religions and that priests, ministers and rabbis love one another like brothers.

They would likely make an exception in his case and not insist on his submitting a script of his broadcast, especially as he would protest and guarantee that he would strictly confine his broadcast to the preaching of His Own Gospel.

Pope Pius XII, seated before his radio in Rome, dressed like his attendant scarlet-robed curia cardinals in his richest regalia, would await Christ's address in high expectation that at last the prerogatives of the Church of Rome would receive the explicit approbation of the Founder of Christianity. So would all his bishops and archbishops throughout the world. Many would gather the faithful into their cathedrals (as when the pope broadcasts from the Vatican) and preside, mitered and enthroned in splendor, before their high altars. For surely they could expect Jesus Christ to do no less than his Vicar in Rome and grant them very special powers to impart the most wonderful indulgence of all time to their poor sinful people!

Despite his promise to the censorship committee not to say a word not already recorded in His Gospel, I would venture to say that the fine sense of humor that I have always imagined Jesus Christ to possess would urge him to preface his Gospel sermon by the following announcement:

"The contents of this speech are by no means fictitious, and any resemblance to characters living or dead is NOT coincidental."

Then, without further ado, would roll out his sonorous verses to be found beginning with the 23rd chapter of St. Matthew's Gospel:

"The Scribes and the Pharisees sit in Moses' seat;

"All therefore whatsoever they bid you observe (about God's law); that observe and do; *but do not ye after their works: for they say, and do not.*

"For they bind heavy burdens and grievous to be borne, and lay them on men's shoulders; but they themselves will not move them with one of their fingers.

"But all their works they do for to be seen by men; they make broad their phylacteries, and enlarge the borders of their garments . . . "

(*Here the chasubled ecclesiastics would fidget with their ermine palliums and richly-embroidered copes, self-consciously withdrawing their bejeweled buckskin slippers under their broadlaced albs*)

"And love the uppermost rooms at feasts, and the chief seats in the synagogues . . .

"And call no man your father on earth: for one is your Father, which is in heaven."

(*Here the pope would glance at the signature he had affixed a while ago to the encyclical letter on his desk and read:*

"PIUS P. P. XII"

the "P. P." meaning "Pater Patrum," "Father of Fathers.")

The voice of Christ coming through the radio would now have become more vibrant, stronger in tone:

"But woe unto you, scribes and Pharisees, hypocrites! for ye shut up the kingdom of heaven against men: for ye neither go in yourselves, neither suffer ye them that are entering to go in."

(*Here the pope would glance nervously at the crossed keys of the kingdom of heaven, symbol for centuries of his office, outlined in costly mosaics on the ceiling above him.*)

"Woe unto you, scribes and pharisees, hypocrites! for ye devour widows' houses, and for a pretence make long prayer; therefore ye shall receive the greater damnation.

"Woe unto you, scribes and pharisees, hypocrites! for ye compass sea and land to make one proselyte, and when he is made, ye make him twofold more the *child of hell* than yourselves.

"Ye blind guides, which strain at a gnat and swallow a camel . . .

"Woe unto you, scribes and pharisees, hypocrites! for ye are like unto whited sepulchres, which indeed appear beautiful outside, but are within full of dead men's bones of all uncleanness.

"Even so ye also outwardly appear righteous unto men, but within ye are full of hypocrisy and iniquity.

"Wherefore, behold I send unto you prophets and wise men, and scribes, and some of them ye shall kill and crucify; and some of them ye shall scourge in your synagogues, and persecute from city to city . . ."

Then, with softened voice, would come his call to the people, entreating them as he did two thousand years ago by the sea of Galilee (*Matt.* 11: 28) :

"Come unto *Me*, all ye that labour and are heavy laden, and *I* will give you rest."

And again to the people before closing:

"*Ye shall know the truth, and the truth will make you free.*"

CHAPTER TWENTY-THREE

THE FELLOWSHIP OF HIS SUFFERINGS

*"That I may know Him, and the power of His resur-
rection, and the fellowship of His sufferings."*
(Philippians 3:10).

NO HEALTHY SOUL deliberately elects to
suffer. To do so would indicate a sickly mind
and distorted spiritual values. Such an unwholesome
attitude of mind and spirit, however, is revealed in
the lives of many "saints" venerated by the Roman
Catholic Church. Suffering in itself is not good or
beneficial, yet it is even extolled by the Catholic
Church as being meritorious, and has led to the de-
grading extravagances and excesses of self-inflicted
torments, heathen flagellations, scourgings and physical castigations with which the catalogue of Roman
Catholic saints abounds. This morbid desire for fleshly
suffering has even descended to such revolting spectacles as that of St. Rita carrying worms in her forehead. Here are a few excerpts from the story of her
life, officially endorsed by the highest Roman Catholic
authorities.[1]

"Making of His crown of thorns, so to speak, a
bow, and of one of the thorns, an arrow, Jesus fired

[1] *The Life of St. Rita of Cascia,* translated by Rev. Dan. J. Murphy,
O. S. A., from the Spanish of Rev. Joseph Sicardo, O. S. A., *cum
permissu superiorum,* N. J. Murphy, O. S. A., Provincial; *Nihil Obstat,*
J. F. Green, O. S. A., *Censor Libr.; Imprimatur,* George W. Mundelein,
D. D., Archbishop of Chicago. 1916.

it at the forehead of St. Rita with such an impetus and force, that it penetrated the flesh and bone, and remained fixed in the middle of the forehead, leaving a wound that lasted all her life, and even to this day, the scar of the wound remains plainly visible. . . . The pain caused by the wound increased day by day, the wound itself assumed so ugly and revolting an appearance, that St. Rita became an object of nausea to some of the nuns" (p. 114).

"So great was her patience amidst all the pain she suffered, that she called the little worms which were generated by the putrid humor of her wound—'her angels'—for they increased her sufferings whenever they moved or fed themselves on her tender and aching flesh, thus giving her new occasions to practice patience and to merit more and more the love and esteem of her divine Spouse, Jesus Christ" (p. 115).

"She suffered continually the most acute and excruciating pains, which were augmented not only by the strong offensive odor that came from the wound, but also by the little worms which dwelt in the wound. St. Rita suffered all with unspeakable patience, and whenever any of the little worms would fall to the floor, she would pick them up with care and replace them in the wound, so that she might suffer more and more. . . . St. Rita suffered with much joy the torments the little worms caused, and, one day, being asked what were those little worms that appeared in her wound, she responded with a smile, saying: 'They are my little angels' " (p. 121).

"Besides the pain of her illness, she suffered the torments of the wound on her forehead, and these torments were made more poignant by the continual movements of the little worms which had also increased in number" (p. 123).

(St. Rita in death): "The little worms which had, indeed, helped to make the countenance of St. Rita abominable were changed into agreeable and pretty lights which twinkled like little stars, and the wound caused by the thorn shone with the brilliancy of a ruby" (p. 132).

Such self-induced torment is not the solution of the problem of pain and suffering given us in the new Christian way of life. All must suffer, but no amount of suffering by any creature can take away or atone for sin. Christ alone, by His sufferings and death, was able to do this for us. All that we can do is to join our whole life, with its joys and sorrows alike, to that of Christ, and to submit our will to God's will.

The will of God is always the choice of the surrended soul, whether it means to abound or to be abased. The full result of this choice, however, has always been that, in so far as the Christian has remained true to the testimony of Jesus, he has likewise gone without the camp bearing His reproach. This is a separation *to* the will of God, not a separation *from* man. It is not manifest in hiding in a cloister, or in donning funereal garments. Grave clothes keep one in bondage, and Lazarus, the risen man, is not to wear them. The Christian is in this world, the scene of Christ's rejection, as a pilgrim and a stranger. His career is a constant vigil and a perpetual fast, but before men he assumes no semblance of fasting. Our Lord, in appearance and dress, was so much like other men, that it was necessary for Judas and the chief priests to arrange a sign between them to determine which one was Jesus. Our fellowship with His sufferings is characterized by our own unobtrusiveness.

Moreover, it is not the cross in itself which is the Christian's choice—again it is God's will. As it was with Simon, the Cyrenian, whom they did *compel* to bear the cross, so with every true Christian there is a divine compelling, and he will find the cross laid upon him. It then becomes his own and he must take it up daily. By denial of self in union with Christ in the fellowship of *His* sufferings, *not ours*, the soul is subdued and can say with Paul, "I am crucified with Christ." Only as we apprehend ourselves *on the resurrection side of the cross* can we glory in it, for "the power of His resurrection and the fellowship of His sufferings" are linked together. For the joy that was set before Him, our Lord *"endured"* the cross.

To bolster a desperately weak spirituality when spiritual perceptions have grown feeble, much is zealously made of externals, of which symbols of suffering are always greatly favored. The world applauds what contributes to it, and Rome grips the imagination of the world. A dead or dying Christ is a popular symbol for a world that would keep Him in the place of His humiliation. An ascetical garb with penitential trimmings receives the world's applause, for the wearer therewith confesses before the world that the sacrifice of Christ is not sufficient. Flesh longs to plume itself with things suggestive of the spirit. Thus the marvelous which can be seen, not the spiritual that cannot be seen, is magnified in Roman Catholic practice. Such externals as the stigmata, physical marks resembling the wounds of Christ, made on Saint Francis

and certain other saints, are given a foremost place
of honor in its system. But the perfecting of faith is
not to be found in ecstasies, raptures, transports and
outward manifestations.

Human suffering is not an expiation for sin;
neither does it further the work of redeeming mankind, as this pernicious doctrine of Roman Catholicism would have us believe. To suffer as a Christian,
according to the will of God, is a mark of identity with
Christ. He took the reproaches of men and felt the con-
tempt of the world; so ought we, for "all that will
live godly in Christ Jesus shall suffer persecution."
He was defamed and despised, and He said "follow
Me." For His sake this may lead to an abiding loneliness, or to drudgery unrelieved by dramatic overtures,
without acclaim; to multiplied grief; to service press-
ed out of measure with burdens; a sacrificial life
spent seemingly "for nought and in vain"—at least
to all outward appearances. And if the Christian
takes a definite stand because of conscience and righteousness to earnestly contend for the faith once delivered unto the saints, he is placed in a position to be
made a spectacle unto the world and to angels and to
men, a fool for Christ's sake. If he dares go further
and steadfastly resists the prince of this world and of
darkness, who now holds high carnival with spiritual
wickedness in high places, he risks being cast forth as
offscouring. What true saint has not experienced the
terrific onslaught of Satan! The acuteness of suffering as a Christian is determined by the degree of holy
sensitivity we possess to all evil, and this is in turn
dependent upon our intimacy with Christ.

Each true Christian is a member in particular of the body of Christ and as such receives his own peculiar discipline. We cannot choose our own course of discipline for "we are *His* workmanship." We can only submit our will to His will. As living stones, each is polished for His unique setting when the Lord of Glory makes up His jewels. To those who would follow to know the Lord, the fellowship of His sufferings is a matter of advanced and holy discipline. As the Roman Catholic Church has presumptuously assumed other prerogatives of the Holy Spirit, it likewise strives to exert control over believers with its own design of discipline—the unscriptural doctrine of penance. It has been the sad history of the Roman Church that while making much of outward evidences of humility and suffering, it has ever sought to take a high place and to avoid becoming identified with Christ in the fellowship of His sufferings. Its leaders have reigned magnificently as kings in this scene of His rejection.[2]

The Christian is being readied to meet the King of Glory. But only He who came down from the effulgence of that glory knows what pleases Him. As it was with Esther who "required nothing" but what she knew the king was pleased to give her, so the true Christian does not dictate the requisites for his particular preparation. For each soul, however, the "oil of myrrh," the fellowship of His sufferings, is as necessary and essential as the "sweet odors."

------

[2] The thought here of course is of the Roman Catholic Church *as a system*, for down through the ages countless individuals in that system have walked with Christ.

For "if we suffer, we shall also reign with Him"
... and so, not by designing our own sufferings, but in
accepting whatsoever is His will, shall we delight the
heart of the King. *"Rejoice, inasmuch as ye are par-
takers of Christ's sufferings, that when His glory
shall be revealed, ye may be glad also with exceeding
joy."*

CHAPTER TWENTY-FOUR

WHAT THE POPE REFUSES TO BELIEVE

WHEN ROMAN CATHOLICS say to me they cannot believe that they can be saved completely and without the ministrations of their priests, I think back to the time when I too, as a priest, could not believe it. Like Martin Luther struggling to find the light, I thought of God's righteousness as a punitive righteousness. And like Luther I wondered in despair how God could expect me to become righteous, and make others righteous, by the works of my own hands.

Luther's discovery of the correct interpretation of the 17th verse of the first chapter of Paul's epistle to the Romans, touched off the spark that set the Protestant Reformation going. He read there about *"The Gospel of Christ . . . for therein is the righteousness of God revealed from faith to faith: as it is written, the just shall live by faith."*

No conversion of priest or layman from Roman Catholicism is complete without full acceptance of the fact here set forth, that the Gospel of Jesus Christ reveals that through faith in Jesus Christ man is actually invested with the very righteousness of God.

Like all other priests who have been converted to the Gospel teaching, Luther had believed, as he was taught in Roman Catholic theology, that this righteousness was solely an attribute of God which man

177

could never attain, and which God held like a big stick over his head.   For this reason he accepted the Gospel as a system of modified law under which salvation had to be earned by good works.

Two other Scripture passages clearly confirm Luther's discovery. The first is *Romans* 3: 21: *"But now, without the law, the righteousness of God is manifested . . . righteousness by faith of Jesus Christ unto all, and upon all them that believe."*   And again, in *Phil.* 3: 9: *"Not having mine own righteousness, which is of the law, but that which is through faith in Christ, the righteousness which is of God through faith."*

Now, it is obvious that this "righteousness of faith" must mean that justifying righteousness with which we are *invested* by God through faith.   It cannot mean the *attribute of righteousness in God himself,* which is an abstract thing, and which obviously is not possessed by God from faith or anything else, since it is inherent in Him by His divine nature.   It comes to us *instrumentally* from faith, however, not from works.   Paul describes it in the Greek as springing out of or from faith—*ek pisteos.* It is *put on us* by God, and is in every sense His work and gift.

Roman Catholics cannot understand how this is possible, because they are never taught to believe that salvation and justification can come to them in any other way except it is *earned* by conforming to the laws of the Church.   This is the old pagan Roman principle that salvation must be earned piecemeal, the same as a salary or reward for proportionate work done by slaves for a master.

It must be remembered that the apostle Paul wrote this epistle about this *new* teaching of the Gospel to *Romans* in Rome itself. They knew of the pre-Christian religious principle of having to earn one's salvation by works. If what Paul told them was in no way different from what they knew and saw around them, why should he want to explain it at all? His object was to show the Romans *by contrast* how much the Gospel teaching differed from the Roman principle of being justified by obedience to external law.

It is also necessary to explain further to Roman Catholics, as Paul did to the Romans of his day, that the actual act of faith, from which the righteousness of God comes, is not in itself anything that is meritorious, any more than other human acts are. A rope cast into the water is the instrument by which a drowning person who grasps it is saved. Faith is similar to the act of the hand that grasps the proffered aid. Paul brings this out farther on, in the fourth chapter of this epistle to the Romans, where he expressly contrasts *faith* with *works* of righteousness: *"To him that worketh not, but believeth on Him that justifieth the ungodly, his faith is counted FOR righteousnesss."* Far from faith being the meritorious root of righteousness, he makes it clear that, on the contrary, it is merely *imputed for* righteousness.

In other words, it has pleased God to attribute a value to faith which intrinsically it has not in itself. It is in a sense similar to what the Government does when it makes a piece of paper into a $100-bill by its official stamp of authority. The piece of paper thus obtains a conventional value which intrinsically it has not.

It is strange, tragic in fact, that the apostle Paul explained all this clearly for the Christian Church in Rome, and *yet the Roman Church today refuses to accept it or teach it to the millions of people under its dominion throughout the world.*   Instead, it holds on to the opposite teaching of salvation by works as it existed in Rome before the Gospel was preached there by Paul.   By so doing, it completely rejects the very pith and center of the whole Gospel message of "righteousness derived from faith" (*dikaiosune ek pisteos*), as Paul puts it, and thus robs its people of the knowledge of the Gospel of Christ, which is "the power of God unto salvation" and their spiritual birthright.

CHAPTER TWENTY-FIVE

THE ROMAN CATHOLIC CHURCH AND MARRIAGE

ALTHOUGH MARRIAGE in democratic countries has been definitely established on a universal civil contract basis, the Catholic Church still claims control over the marriages of all Christians. It insists that the validity of a marriage contracted by any two Christians depends upon Catholic Church law and is not determined by the civil state, the minister, nor even by the parties themselves. So absolute is this control claimed by the Church of Rome that it makes marriage more a contractual pledge binding the two persons to the Catholic Church than a free, mutual, and inviolable contract between each other.[1]

In the centuries preceding the Reformation, the validity and legality of marriage in European countries did actually depend upon Catholic Church approval. The civil law of the nations recognized no form of marriage other than that entered into before a duly authorized priest of the Church of Rome. Nor were other witnesses to the ceremony besides the priest required. Thus, a runaway couple in those days

---

[1] There is here clear evidence how much Catholic Church preaching may differ from conduct; the Catholic catechism defines the very *essence* of marriage as follows: *The whole essence of the marriage contract consists in the surrender by the persons of their bodies to each other, and by declaring by word or sign that they make this surrender, and take each other for husband and wife for now and forever."*— Catechism of Christian Doctrine, by order of the Third Plenary Council of Baltimore, p. 220, Q. 1009.

181

could steal up to the house of the village pastor on a moonlit night, throw a few pebbles at his bedroom window and, when the priest popped out his head, pronounce their marriage vows and depart legitimate man and wife.

After the Reformation the Council of Trent, in an effort at marriage reform within the Catholic Church, laid it down by its decree *Tametsi* that at least two witnesses besides a priest were required. But this decree did not apply in Protestant countries (including many parts of the United States), where the Catholic Church still regarded Catholic marriages as valid which were performed in the presence of a priest alone, and where Protestant unions were not recognized at all as truly Christian marriages. Pope Pius IX declared Protestant and civil marriage, that is, without the Catholic sacrament, "shameful and abominable concubinage".[2]

. It was only in the year 1908, that the Catholic Church, by the decree *Ne Temere* of Pope Pius X, consented to regard marriages of Protestants as valid. This concession, however, is still withheld from Roman Catholics, or a Catholic and a Protestant, who contract marriage before a Protestant minister or a civil marriage officer. Such action is styled an "attempted" marriage in Catholic law and is counted as both illicit and utterly void. This decree aroused great resentment in this country at the time. The following is from a letter to the *New York Tribune* of March 19, 1908:

[2] Allocution, Sept. 27, 1852; *cf.* Raulx, *Encycliques et documents*, Vol. I, pp. 273-4.

"By the laws of the State of New York such marriages are declared to be lawful and binding. The edict declares them to be null and void. In effect, it decrees as illegitimate the matrimonial relations sanctioned by the State, brands the offspring as illegitimate, and by inexorable logic dissolves the marriage bond in such cases without authority of the civil courts. A Catholic, after marriage to a non-Catholic by other than a Catholic priest, may, under this decree, repudiate his wife and marry another with the priestly blessing. . . ."

It was this decree that stipulated the conditions under which alone a Protestant may be permitted to marry a Catholic. It obliged both the Catholic and Protestant party to sign a pre-nuptial agreement: (1) that the marriage shall be performed only before a duly authorized Roman Catholic priest; (2) that all children born of the marriage shall be baptized and educated as Roman Catholics; (3) that the Catholic party to the marriage shall endeavor to induce the other to relinquish the Protestant faith and become a Roman Catholic. Such marriages, furthermore, can only take place in the church rectory or in a private house and not in the church proper; neither can the solemn nuptial blessing be given such a couple.

In Protestant parts of the United States and the English-speaking world, only a few Catholics troubled themselves to obtain a dispensation to marry Protestants under such conditions. The result was that the Catholic Church refused to admit that they were validly married and their children legitimate, and so they were lost to the Church. Furthermore, many who signed the required conditions to contract marriages with Protestants disregarded them afterwards, and so their children were lost to the Church. In order to remedy this, the Holy Office of the Inquisition issued a more drastic decree in January, 1932, which declared, in effect, that if the conditions were not faithfully adhered to, then the dispensation must be counted as "null and void." Thus, if the parties now to a mixed marraige fail to have their children baptized and educated in the Roman Catholic religion, their marriage is automatically dissolved as far as the Catholic Church is concerned. Following is this latest decree of the Holy Office:

"It sometimes happens that so-called mixed marriages between Catholics and non-Catholics, baptized and non-baptized, are contracted, even after the required assurances, but in such a manner that their observance, especially as regards the Catholic education of the children of both sexes, cannot be effectually insisted upon, because, in some regions, where there exist contrary civil laws, it can be prevented both by lay authority and heretical ministers, even against the wishes of parents.

Lest such a grave law, which is both of the divine and natural order, be frustrated with great detriment to innocent souls, the Most Eminent and Most Reverend Cardinals who are appointed to safeguard the integrity of faith and morals, in plenary session held on Wednesday, January 13, 1932, having in mind the recent Encyclical of Our Most Holy Father entitled *Casti Connubii*, decided that it was their strict duty to notify and make it a matter of conscience binding upon all Bishops and Vicars and all those referred to by Canon Law 1044,[3] who have the faculty of dispensing from the impediment of mixed religion and disparity of worship, that this dispensation must never be granted unless the persons to be married first give assurances whose faithful execution no one may be able to prevent, even by the power of the civil laws to which one or other of the parties is subject in his present place of residence, or in any future place, if it can be foreseen that he is about to change his place of residence. *Otherwise the said dispensation is null and invalid."*

This was confirmed and made law by Pope Pius XI on the following day:

"On Thursday, the 14th of the same month, Our Most Holy Lord Pius XI, by divine Providence Pope, confirmed this resolution, and ordered it to have the force of public law, commanding all whom it concerns to observe it and have enforced.

(signed) A. Subrizi,

Supr. S. Cong. S. Officii Notarius."

Fearing trouble with the civil law in democratic countries, priests in general made no immediate effort at legal enforcement of the signed conditions to a mixed marriage. It was doubtful if the simple form of agreement as originally drawn up would have been upheld by the civil law. Protestant public opinion in the United States was also definitely aroused against it. The Federal Council of Churches in America put themselves on record against it as follows:

---

[3] This Canon refers to death-bed marriages, thus making it so that, if the patient recovers, and fails to carry out the conditions, he again becomes not-married.

"Religion is a basic interest in human life, and differences of religion, if these are fundamental, may strain a marriage to the point of breaking, especially when they are aggravated by ecclesiastical interference. No religious body which confesses itself Christian can tolerate the imposition upon one of its own members of the requirements of another religious body by which the religious scruples of that member are aroused, or action repugnant to reason and conscience is forced upon him by an authority which he does not acknowledge . . . If either partner enters upon the union as a progagandist, determined through the intimacies of marriage to subvert the religious faith of the other, disaster is imminent." [4]

But the Inquisitional decree of 1932 left the Catholic bishops of America no alternative. It solemnly bound them to find a way to have the agreement so executed that the conditions could be enforced by the civil law; else to nullify marriages between Catholics and Protestants, even when contracted by dispensation, if the conditions are not carried out after the children are born. In order to meet the situation, therefore, a form of ante-nuptial contract has been devised in some places which gives the Archbishop or his representatives the legal right to enforce each and every one of the conditions signed by the Protestant and Catholic parties to a mixed marriage should either or both of them subsequently fail to carry them out.

Such marriages thus become, in actual fact, a three-cornered affair between the two parties to be married and the archbishop. The contracts are so

---

[4] cf. *N. Y. Times*, Mar. 3, 1932.

drawn up that the young couple may be said to have to get married to the archbishop as well as to each other. For if they fail to carry out the contracts, he can dissolve the marriage.

So complete is the claim of the Roman Catholic Church over everything connected with the marriage of all Christians, that it is safe to say there is no marriage that cannot be made valid or invalid by decree of the Roman Rota. Even marriages of two Protestants, contracted before a Protestant minister, are held to come under the jurisdiction of the Roman Catholic Church.

It was the Roman Rota, in 1926, that finally decided that the marriage of Consuelo Vanderbilt to the Duke of Marlborough, though they were both Protestants and had been married for seventeen years and had several children, was never a true marriage. The reason given was undue pressure on Miss Vanderbilt by her mother at the time of her marriage to the Duke. When the Roman Catholic bishop's court in London had refused annulment on this plea, because it was proved that the Duchess later had given full consent both to continue the marriage and to have children, the Roman Rota reversed the decision of the lower ecclesiastical court of the Bishop of London. The shrewd theological casuists in Rome fabricated a most absurd reason to declare that the parties were never really married. They admitted that, according to their own Canon Law, a marriage originally entered upon under pressure of force or fear, becomes valid if the party thus forced afterwards renews consent freely —as happened in the Vanderbilt case. But these theo-

logians, determined to find some excuse that would
leave the Duke of Marlborough free to marry a Roman
Catholic woman (with the possibility of the Duke himself becoming a Roman Catholic), pompously declared
that the Duchess of Marlborough was only a woman,
and that *theological knowledge was not to be presumed
in a woman ("scientia theologica non est presumenda
in feminis)."* She either knew the effect of this ruling in Roman Catholic theology or she did not, these
learned theologians argued. If she did, she was not
supposed to; if she didn't, she didn't. In either case,
therefore, they concluded, the ruling did not apply in
her case, and so they declared that Miss Vanderbilt
was never at any time married to the Duke of Marlborough and that he was free to enter another marriage with the blessing of the Roman Catholic Church.
Pope Pius XI applauded their verdict and declared
that their decision upheld the sanctity of marriage!

The Roman Rota also favored Marconi, the in-
ventor of wireless telegraphy, in a similar manner.
It went to great lengths to prove that Marconi, a Protestant who married his first wife, also a Protestant,
in a Protestant church in London, had lived in sin
with her during their long married life. He was married in Rome to his second wife, the 18-year old daughter of a papal count, in a splendid ceremony attended
by the highest prelates and dignitaries of the Roman
Catholic Church. In return for the favor, Marconi
built and made a present to Pope Pius XI of the Vatican radio station. If all marriages were judged by
like theological reasoning, few would be found secure.
It is well known that in the peasant parts of Ireland

and Europe, girls are not free to choose their husbands, but are forced by their parents and the priest to marry for monetary and family considerations.

Little interest, however, is shown by Catholic Church authorities in the marriages of the common people. Great pains are taken to satisfy the Vanderbilts and the Marconis; little or none to cure the evils of concubinage and illegitimacy so prevalent in Rome itself. It is reliably reported that thousands of couples in the pope's own parish of St. John Lateran live together and have children without having been married either by church or civil ceremony. Under Italy's parliamentary government, before Mussolini's Fascist regime came to power, the Catholic Church condemned as invalid all marriages of Catholics contracted according to the civil law. The civil law, on the other hand, refused to recognize marriages as valid which were contracted only before a priest. In his concordat with Pope Pius XI in 1929, Mussolini agreed to recognize canon law marriages, that is, the validity of marriages contracted according to the laws of the Church and before a priest alone, together with State sanction of the Church's regulations concerning annulments, birth control, impossibility of divorce, etc. Thus, under the Fascist State in Italy, the medieval control of the Catholic Church over marriage was to all intent and purpose restored.

Despite the obvious evils of divorce in modern democratic countries today, the denial of the right to women in Catholic countries allied to dictatorships to divorce adulterous husbands breeds even greater evils. The number of divorces in democratic countries is no greater than the number of unfaithful husbands in Catholic authoritarian countries where the Church's prohibition against divorce is upheld by the civil law. In such countries there is no check on the waywardness of men and no recourse to the law by wives to obtain either freedom or support from adulterous husbands.

In Latin Catholic countries especially, the priests have always indulgently ignored the traditional custom of married men having one, if not many, mistresses, but have always fought relentlessly against divorce, by which wives could free themselves from such men. The result is a very high rate of illegitimacy in such countries as compared to Protestant countries. This can be seen from the diagram on the opposite page.

Safeguarding of property rights, social status and legitimacy, has always been considered of greater importance to the Roman theologians than individual morality. This accounts for the extraordinary high rate of illegitimacy in Catholic countries such as Italy, Spain, Portugal, France and all Latin American countries. It also provides a convenient excuse for the sex-laxity on the part of the Church's own celibate priests, whose illegitimate children and mistresses suffer from the same disadvantage as those of other men.

The extent of the power claimed by the Catholic Church over marriage can be judged from its extraordinary dispensation entitled, *Sanatio in radice*—literally, "healing from the root." It means that the Catholic Church may remake a marriage, from its

In Catholic Latin American countries, as shown in the diagram below, the rate of illegitimacy is abnormally high—ranging from 25% to 50%. North of the Rio Grande, in Protestant democratic countries, even though it includes Catholic Canada, the rate is only 2.4%

ILLITERACY 6%

ILLEGITIMACY 2.4%

Two Continents!
One Bible!

The white and black portions of the two American Continents shown here were discovered and colonized at about the same time. Any difference of opportunity or of resources that may have existed between them was in favor of the southern Continent. However the northern land prospered greatly from the very beginning in all those things that make life worth while. The southern countries grovelled for four centuries, and still grovel, in almost universal destitution, illiteracy and illegitimacy. WHY? The answer is clear. The countries above the Rio Grande were given the Bible and the Protestant faith of the Pilgrim Fathers. Those to the south were given the sword of the Spaniard and the idols of the priests of Rome. The map tells the rest of the story!

Neglected
Opportunity

The percentage shown for the countries north of the Rio Grande would be even lower were it not for Roman Catholic Quebec in Canada, and the foreign-born Romanists in the United States. The figures for the Latin American countries are, on the whole, approximate, due to the fact that some of of the more backward nations down there do not keep careful records of vital statistics. However, the percentages given are those of the most conservative estimates from authoritative sources.

ILLITERACY 60 TO 80%

ILLEGITIMACY 25 TO 50%

very foundation or root, without the knowledge or consent of one, and sometimes of both parties concerned. For instance, if two people are living together but not properly married according to the laws of the Catholic Church, or even according to the natural law of God, their parents or some interested party can get the priest to arrange that the marriage be made valid unknown to one or both of them. It is secretly granted, usually to favored individuals or to others in extraordinary circumstances, and depends entirely on the will of the bishop who keeps record of it in his secret archives. It is of great advantage to the Church in pleasing influential or wealthy parents of a son who has contracted a civil or Protestant marriage with a Protestant girl and whose parents, on her side, stubbornly refuse to have the marriage done over again before a Catholic priest.

During my years as a priest, I obtained this *sanatio* in three cases, not without protest on behalf of many others who had equal rights to this procedure, but who were left 'living in sin' by the bishop's refusal to apply this dispensation equally to all who needed it. In Protestant parts of the United States, a very high percentage of Catholics marry Protestants in a Protestant church and their marriages are thus regarded as mere 'concubinage' by the Catholic Church. It is impossible to make such people see the need of getting married again by a Catholic priest in order to make their union lawful in the eyes of God. But the bishop has it in his power to apply the dispensation of *sanatio* in such cases and thus make them lawful and valid unions. Yet, despite his belief in this power, he can sleep at night with conscience undisturbed by the fact that by refusing to use this power he keeps thousands of his people living in a perpetual state of mortal sin.

Needless to say, this mandatory power to declare a marriage valid or invalid by consent of a bishop, and without knowledge or consent of the parties concerned, destroys the very essence of marriage. For even the Roman theologians admit that the essence of marriage consists in the free consent of the individuals themselves, limited only by the law of God in their nature.

But the Catholic Church goes farther, and holds that a marriage which is even against the law of God and nature can be validated by special permission of the Roman Rota. In this way even a marriage between brother and sister may be allowed. There is even one case on record, strange though it may seem, where Roman Catholic Church authorities validated the marriage of a man (without his knowledge) to a woman *who thus became his lawful wife while being at the same time his sister and his daughter*. This, of course, is an extreme case. It was used by my professor of moral theology in Rome to prove how absolute is the power of the Catholic Church over marriage, independently of the civil law, the law of nature and of the parties concerned. This is my apology for stating the following details of the case:

The story began with a young unmarried mother who ran a canteen back in the days of the gold rush on the Rio Grande. Her little boy was the idol of her life and she worked and saved for fifteen years to pro-

vide him with an education away from his rude sur-
roundings. She decided to send him to college in Europe to study engineering. Her anguish at the prospect of parting from him for many years was hard to
bear, but she was consoled by the expectation of seeing him come back an accomplished and educated
young man. The night before his departure her maternal longing craved the satisfaction of nursing and
fondling him once again, as she had done when he was
a child in her arms. During that vigil, her maternal
love fused with and was overcome by her natural wo-
manly desire, unknown to her deep-sleeping boy. Next
day he left, and in due time she gave birth to a daughter, whose existence she revealed by letter to her son
only after several years had elapsed. She explained
the little girl by telling him that she was an orphan
foundling whom she had undertaken to care for. It
was twelve years before her son returned, the mother
in the meantime having moved to another locality.

During the years following her son's return, there
grew up between him and this girl an intimate
friendship which the distracted mother could not
deter from ripening into real love. Rather than
expose her shame to her children, the mother
allowed a marriage to take place between them
in Roman Catholic form. But she was soon seized with
remorse and terror, hastened to the priest and confessed the whole story to him. The priest, having no
power to act in such an extraordinary case, presented
the matter, through his bishop, to the Roman Rota,
and this supreme tribunal in Rome, unknown to any
save the priest and the mother, validated the union

by the application of *sanatio in radice*. The identity of the parties being safeguarded, the case was given out to the schools in Rome as proof of the extent to which Roman Catholic control over marriage can be exercised.[3]

Only by its alliance with Fascist, authoritarian regimes can the Roman Catholic Church hope to restore its outworn claims to legislate for marriage and sex by its canon law. In democratic countries its power as marriage legislator has ceased to exist. Restoration of that power would mean denial of the legitimacy of democratic Constitutions, would, in fact, destroy democracy altogether. The very fact of the existence of democratic States, with government of, by and for the people, nullifies such power in any Church. For laws now are made and annulled by the will of the majority of the people, and in democratic countries power over marriage, education and social welfare has been given to governments elected by the people. The voice of the people, not the voice of a pope, king or dictator is now the voice of God.

Yet, in the hope that democracy may some day be wiped out and authoritarianism restored in every country, the Roman Catholic Church persists in con-

---

[3] In Gury's *Doctrines of the Jesuits* (p. 393-4), translated by Paul M. Bert, this same story is told in a slightly different way and begins, in true Jesuit casuistic style, as follows: "Ludimille, a widow of a noble family, who had fallen in a shameful love with her own son, Jules, finds out that during the night he goes to sleep with his servant. She finds a pretext to send his servant away, and slips into the latter's bed. Jules, without the least suspicion, arrives at the appointed time, and unknowingly commits with his mother the most horrible incest. . . " The aim of both versions is the same, namely, to prove that the Roman Rota has the power to validate even such an unnatural marriage as this.

tinuing to legislate for marriage, education and social affairs, even in democratic countries. Such laws are a mere mockery, since they cannot be enforced and therefore are only a cause of sin and evil. From the time of the Council of Trent the marriage laws then enacted have annulled more marriages than they made, since they condemned all marriages, even of Protestants, as invalid that were not contracted according to canon law. Nor did Pope Pius X, in 1908, remedy the situation by his *Ne Temere* decree which *permitted* valid marriages by Protestants in their own churches, not as a matter of right but merely by favor of Roman Catholic authority. For there still remain the vast number of marriages of Roman Catholics who get married by Protestant ministers or by civil ceremony, and whose unions are held to be utterly void and sinful by the Catholic Church. In Protestant parts of the United States, Canada, Australia and South Africa, more than fifty per cent of the Roman Catholics contract civil and Protestant marriages. There was even a higher percentage in so-called Catholic France, Italy, Spain and Portugal before they became Fascist countries.

At bottom, the sole aim of the Catholic Church's attitude toward sex, marriage and birth control is to reach after undisputed control of the bodies and souls of all men. Its whole structure rests upon such control. Humane considerations have little part in its law system. For instance, it makes it a mortal sin for a wife to deny sexual intercourse to a syphilitic husband; requires the sacrifice of a mother's life in dangerous childbirth so that the child may be born alive and baptized a Catholic; will permit no considerations of health, social or economic conditions to interfere with the number of children to be conceived. The spirit of the Christian Gospel, the facts of history, the urge of mankind toward freedom and human betterment, the cry of stricken humanity for its long-delayed right to social uplift and decent conditions of living—all these, if they cannot be fitted in with the claim of the Roman papacy as the sole earthly agent of God, must be sacrificed.

Having possessed itself of the vacated throne of the Roman Caesars, the Catholic Church is still obsessed with the conviction that all men must be ruled to the end of time through a papal agent-of-attorney seated upon a scarlet throne upon one of the seven hills of Rome. *"The kings of the gentiles,"* says Christ, *"exercise dominion over them. But it shall not be so amongst you; but whosoever will be great amongst you, let him be your minister; and whosoever will be chief amongst you, let him be your servant."* (*Matt.* 21: 25-27).

CHAPTER TWENTY-SIX

THE PROBLEM OF MIXED MARRIAGES

"Can two walk together except they be agreed?"
(Amos 3: 3).

C UPID is a capricious sprite and wings his arrows
in odd directions. With increasing frequency
of late, his arrows pin together the hearts of boys and
girls who have been brought up in the religiously
opposing worlds of Roman Catholicism and Protestantism. The warm glow of the physical love of two
such young people for each other blots out for the
moment the importance of their spiritual differences,
and they proceed to plan for marriage and often carry
it through. But soon mountainous difficulties make
themselves apparent, as many have discovered to their
sorrow. There are many obstacles to happiness in
married life, and if religious conflict is added love and
happiness are sure to fly out the window.

In a Protestant democratic country where Roman
Catholics and Protestants live and work side by side
without restriction, the problem of mixed marriages
has become a very real and practical question. At the
root of the problem is the Roman Catholic attitude of
exclusiveness which goes so far as refusal to allow any
of its members to unite in religious worship with
Protestants. The late English Cardinal Bourne,
quoting Margaret Clitherow, England's first "mar-
tyr", put it thus: *"I will not pray with you nor shall
you pray with me; neither will I say 'Amen' to your
prayers nor shall you say it to mine."* No happiness

or unity of spirit can be had between the partners to a marriage union where one of them is schooled in such an attitude of religious bigotry.

Added to this is the Roman Catholic Church's claim to sole jurisdiction over the marriages of *all* Christians. In fact, it condemns every mixed marriage as sinful and invalid unless it is performed by a Roman Catholic priest, and requires the signing of legal contracts that all children will be baptized and brought up as Roman Catholics. It further demands that the Protestant party take six weeks' instruction in the Roman Catholic religion previous to the marriage. After the marriage it requires the Catholic party to exploit the intimacies of marriage so as to induce the Protestant party to join the Catholic Church.

All these claims of the Roman Catholic Church arise from its teaching that marriage is a "sacrament" instituted by Christ and as such within the power of the Roman Church alone to administer. That teaching denies any right either of a Protestant minister or the civil State to legislate for the validity of the marriages of Christians, whether they be Catholic or Protestant. The Protestant view is that marriage, though a very sacred institution, is not a sacrament, since there is no evidence in the New Testament that Christ ever instituted it as such. Protestant teaching holds that marriage is *"an honorable estate, ordained of God unto the fulfilling and perfecting of the love of man and woman."* Protestants consequently do not attempt Church control of it as the Roman Catholics do, and intervene only in cases in-

volving some violation of the clear teachings of Jesus
Christ. In democratic countries the validity of marriage, by the will of the people, rests upon a civil contract basis. Protestants abide by the law in the matter and do not make any attempt to exploit control
of it to increase the wealth and membership of their
church organization as the Roman Catholic Church
does.

There is first the difficulty of the form and manner of the marriage itself. The Roman Catholic
Church will not allow a Protestant minister to be associated in any way with the ceremony, nor will it allow
a priest to assist in a Protestant ceremony. If the
couple is married by a Protestant minister, the Catholic Church condemns the marriage as no marriage at
all and deprives the Catholic party of the sacraments.
Although the marriage is regarded as perfectly legal
by society and the State, the Catholic Church declares
that the couple are living in sin, and as long as they
live together the Catholic party will be refused absolution of any and all sins by the priest. If the Catholic party is a soldier or an airman on the eve of a
dangerous battle and goes to confession to get pardon
of his sins in case he should be killed next day, the
priest will refuse to absolve him unless he promises
to forsake his wife if he comes through safely.

Often, especially when the girl is a Roman Catholic, the Protestant party will submit to the marriage
by a Roman Catholic priest. But even after the contracts have been signed, the marriage cannot take
place in a church. It is performed in the office of the
priest's house and deprived of the glamor of the

Church's ritual which means so much to a Catholic girl. She is also deprived of the nuptial blessing of her Church, and thus in her eyes her marriage falls short of the appearance of a true marriage.

But these difficulties are dwarfed by those that develop in the home that is divided so completely on the matter of eternal salvation. The children reach the age when religious instruction must begin and the Protestant father is forcibly reminded of his signed agreement to allow all his children to be brought up in the Roman Catholic faith. They go off with his wife to one church while he makes his way to another. They are taught that all non-Catholics, including their own father, are deprived of the means of salvation and stand no chance of being saved except in the rare contingency that they are "invincibly ignorant" of the Roman Catholic religion. They are taught a philosophy of life and a code of ethics that outrage his conscience as a good Protestant. Can love and domestic happiness flourish in such a home? Can the romantic love of two people remain steadfast where there is no union of the spirit? In the presence of the great finalities of life that lay bare its harsh realities, that which seems to be union is shown to be no union at all, since souls desperately in need of each other are left separated and alone.

The problem of mixed marriages is one of particular concern to Protestant ministers. Through mixed marriages the souls of their young people are robbed of their spiritual heritage. In most cases it is the Protestant party that yields to the Catholic, since the Roman Catholic Church is a totalitarian institu-

tion that permits no toleration of other religions and
intimidates its members by dire threats of excommunication and forbids them to yield to the rights of
others.   A few brave Protestant ministers, like good
shepherds, go after a sheep that is being led astray
by a mixed marriage and challenge the right of the
Catholic priest to instruct a member of their flocks in
the teachings of the Catholic Church if his Protestant
pastor is not present.   They should go farther than
this and demand the equal right of the Protestant
minister to instruct the Catholic party to a mixed
marriage in the teachings of Protestant Christianity.
Upholders of American law and democratic justice
should also see to it that the validity of a marriage
should not be made dependent upon any particular
form of belief or church ceremony.   It should be made
a felony in the United States, as it is in New Zealand,
for instance, for any Church or individual to declare
or teach that a marriage contracted in accordance
with the requirements of the civil law is not a true
marriage.

Best of all is for Protestant ministers to preach
without ceasing to their people: *"Do not marry a
Catholic. Do not permit yourself to fall in love with
a Catholic, for love is unreasoning and lures its victims into thinking that they are exceptions to all rules
and experiences. Fear of the threats of the Church is
greater than the love which a Roman Catholic girl or
boy may profess for you. This fear will win out in
the end and rob you of your love and happiness as well
as the eternal salvation of yourself and your unborn
children."*

CHAPTER TWENTY-SEVEN

THE REAL CATHOLIC CHURCH OF CHRIST

THE DOGMATIC beliefs and ritualistic ceremonials of the Roman Catholic Church are sustained by a thinly-intellectual veneer, called the Scholastic system of reasoning. Everything taught to and practiced by Catholics is supposed to be proved by the syllogisms of this specialized system of philosophy. It was borrowed from the Greek philosopher Aristotle, but has been so corrupted that it now has only a bare resemblance to what Aristotle taught.

Nothing has contributed more to discredit belief in God and the redemptive work of Christ than this attempt of Roman Catholic theologians to prove them by their trick syllogistic reasoning. It has driven many to atheism or complete agnosticism. Worst of all, it has caused many millions of well-intentioned and sincere seekers after God to lapse into religious indifferentism. Of all the inadequate metaphysical yardsticks to measure the immeasurable immensity of the deity and explain Christ's way of salvation, none is less satisfying and more harmful than the Scholastic syllogism of the Roman Catholic medieval reasoners. It proves nothing beyond what is already known or believed. It begins with the assumption of the proof it pretends to show. It uses the old trick of the stage magician who only takes out of the hat what

203

he first puts into it unknown to the audience. But it
suits perfectly the structure of Roman Catholic law
and theology, since nothing in Catholic teaching and
practice must ever be proved to be different from what
has been already established.   In this way Catholic
Church dogmas remain forever immutable and unquestionable.

No one was more opposed to the absurdity of
trying to convert people to Christianity by trick syllogisms than Cardinal Newman, who is boosted as the
Catholic Church's greatest convert in modern times.
In his *Grammer of Assent* he says:

"Logic makes but a sorry rhetoric with the multitude;
first shoot around a corner, and you may not despair
of converting by a syllogism. Life is not long enough
for a religion of inferences; we shall have never done
beginning if we are determined to begin with proof;
we shall turn our theology into inferences and our
divines into textuaries.   Logicians are more set upon
concluding rightly than upon right conclusions. They
cannot see the end for the process."

Few Roman Catholics know that Cardinal Newman was very unhappy after he became a Roman Catholic. He made honest efforts to awaken Roman Catholics to the need of finding first-hand proof of God's
existence and knowledge of salvation from the Bible.
For this he was distrusted and persecuted by the Roman inquisitors. In his *Life of Cardinal Newman,*
his Catholic biographer [1] quotes from a letter of Newman to H. Wilberforce as follows:

---

[1] *Cf.* Ward's *Life of Cardinal Newman,* Vol. II, p. 252.

"However honest my thoughts, and earnest my endeavors to keep rigidly within the lines of Catholic doctrine, every word I publish will be malevolently scrutinized, and every expression that can possibly be perverted sent straight to Rome. . . " "I shall be fighting," he adds, "under the lash, which does not tend to produce vigorous efforts in the battle, or to inspire either courage or presence of mind."

The chief engineer of this structure of Roman Catholic philosophy was St. Thomas Aquinas, who lived in the thirteenth century. It was he who fixed the teachings of the Roman Catholic Church in their syllogistic moulds, as they are known and used to this day. He gathered together all the beliefs and practices that had developed in the Roman Catholic Church throughout the preceding centuries and tried to prove them all by his special system of medieval reasoning. He called his finished work the *Summa Theologica.* His aim was not to find out the truth about the teaching of Christ as contained in the Bible and New Testament. His task was to find reasons (or excuses) for the beliefs and practices already existing in the Catholic Church and to fix them forever as immutable dogmas that must never be questioned. He sought for conclusions to the logic of words, not for the spiritual power that makes men the children of God through Christ. Like the logicians Cardinal Newman berated, he was more set on concluding rightly than upon right conclusions.

The lack of true spirituality in the religion of Rome to this day can be traced to this juggling of words by Thomas Aquinas to sustain the corrupt practices of the Catholic Church. Like Anselm before him, Aquinas was a clever apologist for the paganization of the Christian religion before his time. He made no attempt to reform the abuses that had multiplied in the Church for over a thousand years. All he did was to brace up the structure of the papacy by the formulations of syllogistic logic. He closed his eyes to the fact that the entire foundation of the Roman religion was corrupted and eaten away. The patch-work of Aquinas made the task all the more difficult for the Protestant reformers, three centuries later, when they set forth to restore the true teachings of Christ to the world. It made it necessary for them to overturn the whole structure of the papacy from its very foundations.

The philosophical formulations of Aquinas' work were concerned particularly with sustaining the main dogmas on which the Roman Catholic Church rests— the sacrifice of the mass, with its doctrine of transubstantiation; purgatory; confession; saint worship, and indulgences. His plan of the Incarnation and Redemption was borrowed from St. Anselm of Canterbury (A. D. 1033). To Aquinas alone goes the praise for the elaboration of such peculiar doctrines as transubstantiation. The very word itself was his own invention. Against all the principles of physical laws, he laid it down that in the mass, the substance of the wafer of bread is transmuted by the words of a priest into the living flesh of Jesus Christ. Neither Aquinas nor anyone who has come after him has ever explained how this happens, or what becomes of the substance of the bread in the wafer. It was something that was believed long before the time of Aquinas, and he found a magic word for it. He reasoned out and proved the other great dogmas of the Roman Catholic religion in the same way. Papal specifications called for an actual *corporeal* presence of Jesus Christ in the wafer of bread. Aquinas made up the formula, into which certain quotations from the Bible were conveniently fitted. His papal masters also called upon him to supply syllogistic formulas to substantiate the Catholic practice of confession and priestly absolution for sins, for the existence of purgatory, and saint worship. Aquinas gave them all they asked for. His magic syllogism, like the prestidigitator's hat, produced them all—because they were all first put into it.

It was this engineering of an unreal and forced alliance of Christianity with the mere chance historical development of power in the Roman Catholic Church that has been responsible for the three great perversions of Christ's true teachings. These three perversions are: *ecclesiasticism, sacramentalism* and *dogmatism*. They are three aspects of the papacy's betrayal of the redemptive work of Christ. They are the three means by which the people have been robbed of religious and civil sovereignty. For these three perversions have sustained religious and civil dictatorship for nearly two thousand years. They destroy the innate rights of the common people to form a true Christian democracy.

Christianity, as rightly taught, can have nothing to do with autocracy of any kind, ecclesiastical or civil. Its development can never be stilted by cramping dogmatism. It is also opposed to sacramentalism, which injects into religion an un-Christlike notion of sacrifice with an accompanying priestly caste.

The teaching of Christ disclaimed all compromise with autocracy, and denied all need of further sacrifice after His universal sacrifice on the cross. The only sacrifice it demands is the collective burnt-offering of all the ignorance, superstition, conventional formalism, of the mass of half-truths and compromise which have heretofore stood in the way of man's liberation. "You shall know the truth," said Christ, "and the truth shall make you free." (*John* 8: 22). Man's redemption and liberation is not a problem that can be solved by metaphysics. If it were it would be unjustly confined to a favored few. Christianity is the spirit of adventure, free to all men in the great open spaces where men congregate. It ought never to have been shut up within the academic circle of the classroom, nor in the choir stalls of cathedrals.

The Christian Gospel proclaimed the good news that a man had been born who was of the same nature as God. Accompanying this message was the assurance that all men might, if they would, share the life of this man, even to the partaking of his flesh and blood. *"As many as received him, to them gave he power to become the sons of God, even to them that believe on his name; which were born, not of blood, nor of the will of the flesh, nor of the will of man, but of God."* (*John* 1: 12, 13).

It was by this road that liberty came into the world, not as the privilege or the accomplishment of superior persons or of any ecclesiastical trust or monopoly, but as the right of every man by virtue of his very humanity. This is the pivotal point of Christianity and of all human history. If a man is just a mere creature of God, the quintessence of dust, he must be ruled, like the animals, forever by external law and dictatorship. In that case, the sovereignty of absolutism, based upon the foundations of economic and defensive necessity, would be irrevocably established. This is what Fascism and Nazism tried to make the world believe, and it is thus no wonder that their contentions were supported by the hierarchy of the Roman Catholic Church.

On the other hand, if it be true, as Christ taught, that a man may become the kin of God, then for a certainty the sovereignty of the people will be established, even though it may take many more centuries of tragedy and failure to make it come to pass. It can never be established, however, by brute force, but only by the free association of enlightened and spiritually consecrated people.

The allotted work of the Christian Church was to attain this end by co-ordinating and 'catholicizing' the wills of the people for their ultimate governance of the world. It had a duty gradually to reduce the economic and police forces to a relation of organic subordination to this ideal. It would in the end abolish forever the infidel empire of *musts* and *must-nots*, since all the people, having been "born again" as sons of God would need no outside force to keep order among individuals or nations. Christianity was therefore intended to establish a universal order in the spirit of democracy, to be, in other words, the genesis of the American ideal.

The fact that Christianity has so far failed in this is the tragedy of history. And the blame for this tragedy rests on the Roman Catholic Church, which has persisted in preserving the absolutism of an imperial Christianity. In the beginning, it took the place of the decayed Roman Empire, and acted as the necessary carrier-body of man's redemptive spirit. But it has become a monster in this, that, being only a body, it has usurped unto itself the functions of spirit. Its head, the pope, claims to be the mouthpiece of the Holy Ghost and the vicar of Jesus Christ. It naturally could not produce the fruits of the spirit. Instead, it produced, as it only could, the fruits of legalism, externalism and a mere corporate unity welded together by the evil force of papal absolutism. Bound to the Roman *curia*, Christianity could not be expected to bring forth the truth and freedom promised to mankind by its founder Jesus Christ. Truth and freedom are correlative: truth cannot be obtained by force and metaphysical reasoning; neither can liberty be granted by charter of any corporate system.

The modern democratic conception of liberty is nothing newer than the Christian teaching of inalienable individual rights and the mystery and awe of co-creatorship with, and sonship of God. More than ever before, it is now being realized that such an idea of liberty cannot come to terms with any kind of ecclesiastical trust or spiritual monoply. Only recently have thinking people begun to understand that real liberty cannot be created by any system of government or legal corporate entity; that it can never be a thing hammered into shape by obscure, undefined termino-

logy and clamped down upon people in the mass. They
are beginning to see that not upon the fixity of philosophical and theological codes, but upon the sound relations of a lot of private individuals to the universe
as made by God, can the expectations of the coming
justice and beauty for men on earth be realized.

Liberty can only be built up synthetically by
units, by individuals brave enough to find God for
themselves; who do not try to shift the responsibility
for their salvation to priests of any Church; who are
courageous enough to reject the claims of priests that
the Church is a kind of 'spiritual insurance society'
that can guarantee them against loss of salvation in the
next world; who are fully convinced that there is no
human person or power, religious or legal, that is able
to assume their souls. This liberty will increase when
enough people fully understand that God has appointed no earthly agents with power of attorney to act
for him, and that the only true sovereignty is in their
own souls, not in those who sit on the thrones of kings
or popes. In spite of all its grandiose claims, a Church
system like the Roman papacy can excommunicate
but can never exclude from salvation; the State likewise can execute, but cannot convict. A true Christian obtains the grace of salvation by himself through
Christ; the sinner convicts himself by his own crimes.

The Roman Catholic Church is irrevocably bound
to its medieval philosophical and theological code,
which denies this conception of liberty. Its autocratic, juristic system is the enemy of every true witness
of this spirit of liberty the moment he attempts to
assert it. Christian democracy therefore cannot stop

even to argue with the Roman papacy. Nor should it fear its threats or hesitate to prevent repetition of its political intrigues with those who, even after the defeat of Fascism and Nazism, may still try to rob the common man again of hard-won religious, economic and civil liberties.

For a fuller treatment of the development of Christianity into the communal ideology of modern democracy, see *The Religion of Democracy*, and *The Affirmative Intellect*, by Charles Ferguson, published by Funk & Wagnalls Co., 1906.

CHAPTER TWENTY-EIGHT

THE 'A-TO-Z' OF SALVATION

"I am Alpha and Omega."—Rev. 1: 8.

THE FINAL MASTERPIECE of Christian imagery is contained in Christ's pronouncement from His throne of glory as found in *Revelation* 1: 8: *"I am Alpha and Omega."* 'Alpha' is the first, and 'Omega' the last letter of the Greek alphabet, and by this simile Jesus, the risen and ascended Saviour, declares: "I am the 'A' and the 'Z,' the beginning and the end, of everything. It is Jesus' self-revelation of His *inexhaustibility,* His *indispensability,* His *efficiency* and His *adaptability.* Above all, it is final proof of the fullness and completeness of His redemptive work. It is the seal that proves Jesus Christ to be "the *author* and *finisher* of our faith."

It began when Moses asked credentials of the Most High to substantiate his august mission to represent God to man. He was told to say, *"I WHO AM hath sent me."* "I am—?" "I am—who?" "I am—what?" It was a magnificent formula, but only a fragment that would be completed in the fullness of time. For thousands of years the question remained unanswered, and the gap that had so long remained blank was filled by Him who repeatedly declared: *"I AM the door;" "I AM the True Vine;" "I AM the Bread of Life;" "I AM the Good Shepherd;" "I AM the Way, the Truth, and the Life;" "I AM the Resur-*

rection and the Life." The sublime climax of it all
was reached when the same Jesus revealed Himself
in the closing stanza: *"I am Alpha and Omega."* I
am the 'A' and the 'Z' of it all, the whole alphabet of
creation and salvation.

The significance of this sublime symbolism can
only be fully realized if one considers the inexhaustible wealth of literature contained, for instance, within
the twenty-six letters of our alphabet. I have discovered that it takes eighteen million cards to catalogue the names alone of all the books in the New York
Public Library. Yet between the covers of this mountain of books you will find simply the twenty-six letters of the alphabet, arranged and rearranged in
kaleidoscopic variety or juxtaposition. You will find
Shakespeare's *Romeo and Juliet, Hamlet* and *Mac-
beth;* Dickens' *David Copperfield, Oliver Twist* and
The Pickwick Papers, and so on. Yet each author,
each poet and novelist, wrote nothing but the twenty-
six letters of the alphabet, shuffled, marshalled, and
set forth in an order they never before assumed. By
doing so, they did not even begin to exhaust the alphabet. The writers of today and tomorrow will find it
as fresh, and unworn, and as ready to their purpose
of creative writing as did the writers of the past.

As Alpha and Omega, the alphabet of all creation
and salvation, *Jesus Christ is infinitely more inexhaustible.* There is neither end nor measure to His
pity, His pardon, His love and, above all, His power.

Like the alphabet, Jesus Christ is also *indispensable.* Literature, with all its hoarded treasures,
is inaccessible until the alphabet is mastered. In this

way also, what the alphabet is to literature, Jesus is to the life of each of us. Without Him, all is a hopeless blank, a baffling enigma, an insoluble mystery. Unless you become acquainted with Him, you cannot enjoy the choicest treasures of life on this earth, nor the radiant raptures of the life to come.

This sublime imagery is also the revelation of the *efficiency* of Jesus. He begins at the beginning with 'A,' and wins out to the very end at 'Z.' He is the *"author* and *finisher* of our faith." Nothing He does can be incomplete or in any way imperfect.

Likewise, this alphabetic parable reveals the *adaptability* of Jesus. Nothing is so adaptable as the alphabet. No two people are alike, nor are their thoughts the same. Yet all men can express their differing individualities through the agency of the same alphabet. The alphabet is the most fluid, the most accommodating, the most plastic device known to man. The lover makes its twenty-six letters the vehicle for the expression of his affections; the poet transforms them into a song that will express the moods of nations and individuals for centuries; the judge on the bench turns them into a sentence of death. By similitude Jesus employs this remarkable quality of the alphabet as an emblem of Himself. He, too, adapts Himself, with divine exactitude, to the individual needs of each of us.

You do not need Jesus in the precise sense that Paul needed Him, or that Augustine, Luther, or John Wesley needed Him. But you need Him in a way all your own. And He can match that peculiar need of each just as the alphabet can lend itself to each writer

and his mood. Until we have discovered the amazing
facility with which Jesus can meet our distinctive
yearnings and needs, we cannot fully appreciate His
power and value as a Saviour. Like the alphabet, He
will adapt Himself to you with the most perfect pre-
cision. He is the very Saviour that *you* and *I* need.

How different is this true teaching about Jesus
as inexhaustible, indispensable, completely efficient,
and wholly adaptable Saviour, to the parody made of
Him by the teachings and practices in the Roman
Catholic Church! There salvation is not free, full or
complete. The things of God are fitted to suit the
ways of men and, as a consequence, result in mere
half-measures. You still need human priests to offer
sacrifice daily for your sins and to be your mediator
with God. By their works you are made not good
enough for heaven and, at best, not bad enough for
hell. They make it so that you die half-saved and can
promise you nothing better than an indefinite period
of punishment, expiation and purgation in the fires
of purgatory. Christ is not allowed to adapt Himself
to your needs; you must adapt yourself instead to the
needs of the human organization of the Church. His
power is not inexhaustible but limited, and you must
depend on the merits of the Virgin Mary and other
"saints," to make up for Christ's insufficiency. The
"finisher" of your salvation is not Christ, but the
priest who has still to offer sacrifice for you even after
you are dead. But since everything is done by the
works of men, no claim is made, nor can it be made,
that any guarantee is given *when* your salvation will
be complete.

No one less than Christ can be your complete and sufficient Saviour. The whole gamut of your salvation, from *A to Z*, is in His hands. He alone is the beginning and the end—the Alpha and Omega—of all creation and salvation.

CHAPTER TWENTY-NINE

CHRIST—THE ONLY ONE

THE PERSON AND WORK of the Lord Jesus
Christ are characterized by such words as *"one,"*
"once," and *"only."* The promises were not made to
Abraham's seed as of many, writes St. Paul, but as of
one, which is Christ.

This unique exclusiveness of the Lord is nowhere
more emphasized than in the words of David in the
Psalm: *"Thou wilt not leave my soul in hell, neither
wilt thou suffer thine Holy One to see corruption."*
The identity of him concerning whom the Psalmist
spoke, and the fact that he was referring to only one,
are clearly verified by the apostles Peter and Paul in
Acts 2 and 13, both affirming that the Holy One who
passed the portals of death and rose again without
seeing corruption, to die no more, is the Saviour, Jesus
Christ. Though He tasted death for every man, it
was impossible for death to hold Him. *In Him was
life!* Only Christ could say: *"I am He that liveth, and
was dead; and behold I am alive forever more."*

All true Christians are called saints (holy ones),
having been made righteous and holy through the
offering of the body of Jesus Christ *once* for all; for
by *one* offering He has perfected forever the sanctified. However, the Lord is the only One inherently
holy in His being—*the Holy One.* "Thou *only* art
holy" is part of the song of the triumphant throng

glorifying the Lord, that St. John heard while on the Isle of Patmos. Hence to admit that *another Holy One* has gone into death and, without returning to corruption, has bodily ascended glorified into Heaven, is to accept strong delusion and a counterfeit from the realm of darkness.

Yet the Roman Catholic Church would have us believe such a cunningly devised fable concerning Mary, the mother of Jesus. To deny the "Assumption of Mary," say they, is impious and dangerous.

Well did St. Paul warn us that, as Eve was beguiled through subtlety, so our minds may be corrupted from the simplicity (singleness) that is in Christ. The technique of Satan is duplicity (double-dealing), and blind guides and idol shepherds fall into his snare to promote another Holy One. He takes the coarse and the base, or the refined and sublime, even the tenderness of mother-love so attractive to our nature—whatever furthers his undeviating purpose —to obstruct man's view of the Lord, and to keep his mind and heart detached from the Person of Christ.

By a masterstroke in spiritual wickedness the name of Mary has been seized upon, and multitudes are kept in bondage charmed and fascinated by a fable.

Meager indeed is the Scripture record of this blessed woman. Nothing is told concerning her after the first chapter of Acts. She is not once mentioned by St. Paul, the teacher of the Gentiles in faith and truth. Does not this silence reprove any curious probing and intruding into the sacredness of God's individual intimacies?   He who knows what is in man and discerns the thoughts and intents of the heart, understands well our frailties, and has given us all the record we should have of Mary.   She who was overshadowed by the power of the Highest, God has been pleased to hide until the time of her exaltation in due season—but every man in his own order: Christ the firstfruits, afterward they that are Christ's at His coming.

The maze of confusion which is tradition is not in agreement as to Mary's death and burial.   Some suppose these events took place at Ephesus, others that they occurred in Jerusalem or Bethlehem.   What matters it!   The single eye is on the Lord!   The attuned ear hears but His voice, and His call is plain: "Follow thou *Me*."   Thus was Peter rebuked when he sought to determine what should befall John and what should be John's lot.   This undue curiosity and over-solicitude in the Lord's dealing with another caused the "turning about" of Peter—*away from the Lord* to better observe John. The eye, no longer single, is turned from the Creator to the creature. How complete is the falsehood of Roman Catholicism, that the worship of Mary honors the Lord.   To this malicious invention from the 'father of lies' our Lord has answered: "Thou shalt worship the Lord thy God, and *Him only shalt thou serve*."   Again says the Psalmist: "*I have set the Lord always before me*," and our jealous God will not permit of another—*He is the only One*.   What became of Mary, the blessed mother of Jesus?   To truly honor the Lord is to heed His rebuke to Peter—"What is that to thee?   Follow thou *Me*."

The Lord Jesus Christ quickeneth all things for He *only* is our life, the *only* wise God, incorruptible, invisible, dwelling in the light which no man can approach unto, and in His times He shall show Who is the blessed and *only* Potentate, the King of kings and Lord of lords.

CHAPTER THIRTY

FIVE BASIC POSTULATES OF PROTESTANTISM

S IMPLICITY is characteristic of the teachings of
Evangelical Christianity—and rightly so. For
it has been well said that multiplication of doctrines
is perilous to the spiritual life. It tends to distract
our attention and, by fixing it upon fragments, dulls
the sense of the immeasurable whole.

This multiplication and fragmentation of doctrines is characteristic of Roman Catholic teaching,
and clearly points up the contrast between it and the
true Gospel teaching.

Following are five points, which may well be
called basic postulates of Protestantism. They not
only clarify all that is necessary and basic to the
Christian teaching about salvation, but show up the
opposing errors of Roman Catholic teaching in each
particular:

1. THE PRIMACY OF CHRIST.

All Protestants base their hope of salvation on the
Gospel teaching that Jesus Christ holds the primacy
in all things—to the exclusion of all others (*Col.*
1: 18). This primacy is manifold: *primacy in the
incarnation*, since He alone took man's nature without sin; *primacy in the all-sufficiency of His sacrifice*
"offered once for all," so that there is now "no more
offering for sin;" *primacy in love and sympathy to-*

ward us, needing no persuasion, no intervention of priest or angel or other intercessor; *primacy also in the honor and glory justly due to Him* and from which nothing can be deducted or accorded to any creature.

Opposed to this is Roman Catholic teaching: that this primacy is shared by men, by the Pope as claiming to possess all power in heaven and on earth; that Christ's sacrifice is not perfect and complete and once offered forever, but must be repeated and even improved upon by priests offering the 'sacrifice' of the mass daily for the sins of men; that love and honor due to Christ must flow exclusively through these priests and other created beings.

2. MAN'S PERSONAL, DIRECT ACCESS TO GOD.

Protestants believe that when a soul is convinced of sin and when guilt presses upon the conscience, reconciliation is had by personal acceptance of Christ's invitation: *"Come unto ME. . . . and I will give you rest;"* that forgiveness cannot be negotiated by the ordinances of a Church or by the absolution of a priest. Roman Catholic teaching says: *"There is no salvation without the priest."* Protestants say: *"There is full salvation in Christ."*

3. A CONSCIOUS SENSE OF PARDONED SIN.

Protestants are logical in expecting from Christ, their Saviour, not a partial, but a full pardon for sin, a pardon that not merely wipes a soul clean just for a time, but that makes the sinner a new creature. They fully believe that: *"There is now no condemnation to*

them who are in Christ Jesus" (*Rom.* 8: 1), that:
"Sin shall not have dominion over you," and that
Christ's work and message bring joy and freedom.

Roman Catholicism, on the other hand, counts it
a sin of presumption to be *assured* of salvation, and
teaches that men must always seek, but will never
find, a profound and blessed sense of full forgiveness
and assurance of salvation. Its saints are distinguished by their misery, not by their happiness. *It
is as if Christ had died in vain.*

4. BELIEF IN THE RIGHT OF PRIVATE JUDGMENT.

Protestants assert the right of each one to find
and judge for himself about the truth of God and
salvation. They also believe in the sacredness of the
personal responsibility that goes with this right. The
Bible to them is an open book, wherein each seeker
after truth can be fully and infallibly enlightened.
They acknowledge that in Christian teaching you cannot transfer to another the responsibility for your
faith, and, if you do so, you thereby weaken your
moral and spiritual character.

In Roman Catholic teaching, the priest takes the
responsibility for the mistakes and sins of his people,
and the Roman Catholic Church becomes in reality a
kind of *'spiritual insurance society,'* to which its members dutifully pay their dues, and onto which they
shove off all responsibility for their sins and their
souls' salvation. Ultimately, all responsibility for
the entire membership rests with one man—the Pope
—since he alone is declared to be the infallible guide
for all.

5. THE BIBLE AS THE WORD OF GOD.

In the Bible all Protestants find the perfect rule of faith and practice. It is to them the Word of God made manifest in their hearts, just as Christ is God made manifest in the flesh of man.

Although the Roman Catholic Church now professes to allow its people to read the Bible, prohibition against any private interpretation of it, that is in any way contrary to the Church's teachings and practices, still remains.

On these five basic postulates, Protestants of all denominations can establish a unity that will more than match the false and merely external unity of Roman Catholicism. But it is not sufficient for Protestants merely to profess these fundamental postulates in words. They must prove them by *demonstrating* their spirit and power.

CHAPTER THIRTY-ONE

EVANGELICAL MOVEMENTS WITHIN THE CHURCH OF ROME

CAN ROMAN CATHOLICS BE SAVED without breaking with their Church? Are there any Evangelical Christian believers within the Roman Catholic Church? These are questions which deserve, and require, extended answers.

It is not generally known that movements toward acceptance of Evangelical Christian beliefs have always existed within the Roman Catholic Church—both before and after the Reformation. Protestants have been so engrossed with the history of their own Church since the Reformation that they know little of the struggles toward the revival of Evangelical Christianity within the Church of Rome since the sixteenth century. Because of this, Protestants today have lost perspective of their own teachings, and a necessary sense of *contrast* between the Gospel teaching which they believe, and the opposite erroneous teaching and practice of Roman Catholicism from which the early Protestants broke away. These early Protestants saw that contrast etched in all its clarity because they knew both sides.

The shining of a bright light on a dark object shows up its true condition. In the same way, the actual doctrinal state of Roman Catholicism is fully seen only when justification of sinners through faith in the finished sacrifice of Christ is definitely and fully preached against the background of the errors of Roman Catholicism. For the main dividing line in the struggle of Roman Catholicism against Evangelical Christianity is drawn between their opposing views as to how the grace of salvation comes to the souls of men. It is upon this ground that the Jesuits have fought their counter-Reformation — not only against Protestants, but also against those who have tried to reassert Evangelical teaching *within the Roman Church itself* after the example of the Protestant reformers of the sixteenth century.

THREE-CORNERED CONFLICT

There have been, in fact, not just *two* but *three* sides to the religious struggle during the four centuries since the Reformation—between Protestantism and Jesuit Catholicism on the one hand, and Jesuit Catholicism and Evangelical factions within the Roman Church itself, on the other. The Jesuits have been as harsh and uncompromising against those who opposed them from within their own Church, as against the Protestants from the outside. It is sad to have to admit that today, there is little, if any, life left in Evangelical movements within the Church of Rome. The Jesuits have succeeded, almost completely, in crushing out the remnants of criticism in the Catholic Church of their teaching about grace and the means of salvation. Their Pelagian doctrine of salvation by works of man himself, with all it implies in their moral theology and devotional practices, is now almost universally accepted or reluctantly acquiesced in by the universal Roman Catholic Church.

The very fury of Jesuit opposition to the Gospel teaching of salvation by faith, as reasserted by Luther, Calvin, and other sixteenth century reformers, has led to the denial today in Roman Catholic teaching of almost every truth upon which the Gospel teaching about the grace of salvation rests.

COUNCIL OF TRENT

But it was not so within the Roman Catholic Church at the time of the Reformation, and even within the Council of Trent itself, which was convened shortly thereafter for the special purpose of resisting the Evangelical teachings of the Protestant reformers. Many Roman Catholic churchmen in that council maintained that the only way to stop Luther and his associates from causing a rift in the Christian Church was *open opposition from the Church of Rome itself against the Pelagian error of the Jesuits, and a firm declaration of salvation full and free by acceptance of the grace of God through the merits alone of Jesus Christ.*

Had these Catholic spokesmen been listened to, the history of Christianity from that day to this would have been different. But the Jesuits triumphed in the Council of Trent on this vital question, as they did in the Vatican Council of 1870 on the question of Papal Infallibility. They have now this latter weapon of undisputed papal power with which to whip everyone—priests, bishops and laity alike—within the

Roman Church into blind acceptance of their peculiar teaching about salvation and their devotional practices.

In the Council of Trent the Archbishop of Sienna, two bishops and five others, fought long and hard against the Jesuits by upholding justification simply and solely by the merits of Christ through faith. The English Cardinal Pole, who presided at the Council in the absence of Pope Paul III, also entreated those assembled not to reject this doctrine simply because it was held by Martin Luther. But the Jesuits— through their spokesmen Lainez and Salmeron—were adamant against even a compromise, and in the end secured adoption of the long list of Tridentine canons and anathemas that were finally pronounced against Protestant Evangelical teaching. Cardinal Pole and the Archbishop of Sienna left the Council in despair. So bitterly has the Jesuit Lainez been hated by *Catholic* anti-Jesuit writers that they have gone so far as to interpret *Rev.* 9: 1, as if he were the fallen star who let loose the scorpion-locusts—the Jesuits—on the world.

RIFT WITHIN CATHOLICISM

But the opponents of the Jesuits in the Catholic Church itself did not submit at once after the Council of Trent. The fight went on, continually at first, intermittently ever since. The Jesuits' chief opponents on the teaching about grace have been the Dominicans, and to this day a wide rift still exists between these two Orders in the Church of Rome, in spite of apparent unity from the outside. The Dominicans

follow their great theologian St. Thomas Aquinas,
who adopted a watered-down interpretation of Augustine's teaching on grace as an entirely free gift of God,
and put it in his medieval syllogistic form.   This is
enough in the eyes of the Jesuits to brand them as
'Calvinistic.'   *Few people today know of this serious
rift within the Roman Catholic Church, or stop to
think that it is actually wider than any doctrinal difference separating the denominations of Protestantism.*

The conflict concerning the nature of grace was
openly continued between the Jesuits and Dominicans
till the end of the sixteenth century, and on into the
seventeenth. In 1596, Pope Clement VIII consented to
hear both sides and promised to give a decision.   *No
less than sixty-five meetings and thirty-seven disputations were held on the subject in his presence.* Pope
Clement himself seems, from his writings, to have
favored the Dominican side, but he put off giving a
decision. The so-called infallible mouthpiece of God
could not decide the most vital question of Christian
teaching, on the question that really matters in the
whole gamut of Christian doctrine: the truth about
how men can be saved!

Pope Clement's hesitation can easily be explained.
The Jesuits by then had become, not only powerful,
but violent and dangerous. They had made themselves the great political prop of the Roman Church
that had been shaken to its foundations in the principal countries of Europe. They went so far as to
threaten the Pope himself, since they counted on having King Henry IV of France on their side. Pope

Clement was also well aware that the political power of the papacy at that time was on the wane, threatened by Protestant England under Queen Elizabeth on one side, and by Protestant Germany, the Netherlands, and Scandinavia on the other. He was advised by the astute French Cardinal du Perron to leave matters as they were, since even a Protestant could subscribe to the doctrines of the Dominicans.

The dispute was continued under Pope Paul V, who became Pope in 1605. *Seventeen meetings were held in his presence, but he too failed to condemn the Jesuits.* Venice at that time was at war with the papacy, and the Jesuits fought so well for the Pope that they suffered expulsion by the Catholic rulers and people of the Venetian Republic rather than yield to the Pope's enemies. It thus seemed more important to the Pope to please the Jesuits than to uphold the most vital doctrine of the Christian Church. In the end Pope Paul issued the Bull *Unigenitus*, in which he promised that a decision would be published "at the proper time," and that in the meantime, neither side was to malign the other. And so it remains to this day in the Roman Catholic Church: *no official decision has ever been made as to how the grace of salvation comes to the souls of men!*

JESUITS VS. DOMINICANS

This was a triumph for the Jesuits, and they have used it to great advantage ever since against both Protestants and those *within* the Roman Church who would dare to dispute their Pelagian doctrine of grace.

They have ruthlessly crushed any priest, bishop or even pope who seemed to veer in any way to the doctrine of the Reformation, namely *that we can do no good works acceptable to God without the grace of God through Christ 'preventing' us; that the will to good, and the works we perform as a result of this good will, are all a free gift of God.*

This was the teaching of Augustine against Pelagius and his followers, which was revived by the Protestant reformers. The Dominicans have always tended to this Augustinian doctrine of grace because St. Thomas Aquinas incorporated some of Augustine's teachings about grace into his *Summa Theologica.* But even the Dominicans never have dared to carry Augustine's teaching to its logical conclusion, as Calvin did, since it would have led to the complete rejection of papal power. The Jesuits have made sure to this day that the Dominicans would never be allowed to go so far. But certain sections of the Roman Church are still accused by the Jesuits as "tainted" with Calvinism because of their advocacy even of the watered-down teachings of Augustine as expounded chiefly by the Dominican theologians.

A particular instance of this may be seen in the fact that most Roman Catholic priests, especially of the Dominican order, who renounce the Church of Rome join up with the Presbyterian Church and ministry. Two examples recently noted by *The Converted Catholic Magazine* are Rev. Dr. George Barrois, formerly a Dominican priest and professor at Catholic University in Washington, D. C., now a Presbyterian minister and Professor at Princeton Seminary, and Rev. J. A. Fernandez, for sixteen years a priest of the Dominican Order, now a Presbyterian pastor in Philadelphia.

The most notable example of the opposition to Jesuit Pelagianism is that of the Jansenists, who publicly professed their belief in the Evangelical teaching of salvation and justification by faith alone in the merits of Jesus Christ, *but who still steadfastly continued within the Church of Rome.* The suffering they endured from the Jesuits, the wonderful example and encouragement they supplied to those within the Roman Church who secretly resented the domination of the Jesuits, should give hope that it may not yet be too late for a second Reformation within the Church of Rome in our day.

JANSENIUS

The Jansenists got their name from Cornelius Jansenius, Bishop of Ypres, who was born in 1585 and died of the plague in 1638, after being bishop for only two years. It was only after his death that his opposition to the Pelagian teaching of the Jesuits became known. But for many years he had made it his business to study the writings of Augustine on the vital subjects of grace, free will and human impotence, original sin, election, faith, etc. Whereas Calvin used Augustine's teaching on these subjects to oppose the whole nature and structure of Roman Catholicism, Jansenius used it only for one immediate object—to check the rising power of the Jesuits and their false teachings within the Church of Rome. His object was not to undermine the Roman Catholic Church as a whole, but to save it from complete corruption in matters of faith and morals.

He put his findings in a book, entitled, *Augustinus,* which was published in Louvain two years after his death and was made the chief weapon by his followers to save the Catholic Church from the evil influence of the Jesuits. For there were many within the Church of Rome at that time who sighed for some real spirituality and who, like Bishop Jansenius, found in the doctrine of salvation by grace, even though only partially and imperfectly apprehended, a great solace and an assurance which the ritualistic observances of the Church of Rome could not supply.

JESUIT OPPOSITION TO GRACE

That was before the blight of Jesuitism had descended completely on the Roman Catholic Church as we find it today. But the Jesuits were then, a hundred years after their Order was founded, rapidly consolidating their power by their lax system of casuistry and other teachings which deadened the conscience. They had by then introduced themselves everywhere as confessors, and had gained great influence by softening all ideas of guilt. Their main purpose was to introduce into Catholic teaching the exclusion of real repentance before God as a prerequisite for forgiveness of sin. In this way salvation would become entirely dependent upon the priest, to the ultimate advantage of the Jesuits themselves—who have always aimed to make themselves the ruling caste of priests in the church of Rome. They have achieved this objective today, and hold the whip hand not only in religious matters, but also as the high political rulers of the Vatican.

What the Jesuits most abhorred, and continue today to abhor, is the true Christian teaching of *justification of sinners through faith in the one finished sacrifice of Christ, and repentance for sin directly toward God.* They were quick to see the danger to their aims in Jansenius' book, *Augustinus*, which upheld this true Christian teaching. They therefore had the book banned, and began by venting their enmity on Jean Baptiste du Vergier de Hauranne—better known as *St. Cyran*, after the monastery of that name of which he was abbot. St. Cyran had secretly studied the doctrine of grace together with Jansenius at Louvain. He was also connected with the celebrated Abbey of Port Royal in France, a community of nuns which had grown very lax in discipline and morals. Yet, it was through this French convent that what is known as "Jansenism" began, and which for almost seventy-five years carried on its remarkable fight to rid the Catholic Church of the perverse teachings and control of the Jesuits.

The cruel methods used by the Jesuits to crush out the Jansenists were equalled only by the atrocities of the Nazi Gestapo in our time. The inmates of Port Royal and their friends were hounded, brutally persecuted, excommunicated, and jailed, because they professed, above all else, the Evangelical doctrines of justification by grace.

PORT ROYAL

There are two things about the nuns of Port Royal and their friends that Protestants and Catholics alike today may well be amazed at. One was that they *persisted in remaining within the Church of Rome while professing absolute faith in the saving grace of Jesus Christ alone.* They strenuously objected to being called Protestants.

The second extraordinary fact is that the abbey of Port Royal, which was to become the great champion of this Evangelical teaching, was so lax in discipline in 1602, that Mother Angelique—under whose later guidance Jansenism thrived there—*was appointed abbess when she was but a girl of eleven years old.* The church authorities in France and her family connived at this, and had her certified as abbess by the Pope, by pretending she was seventeen! [1]

How thoroughly Evangelical the inmates of Port Royal later became—while still remaining within the body of the Roman Catholic Church—may be judged from the story of the last prioress, Mother Dumesnil Courtinaux, as she lay on her dying bed. Port Royal had been finally suppressed and uprooted by the Pope eight years previously, but this last Mother prioress still retained her faith in salvation by grace alone. But she desired to die in good standing in the Catholic Church and begged for the last sacraments. The Bishop of Blois came but refused to administer the

---

[1] See, *The Jansenists, Their Rise, Persecutions by the Jesuits, and Remnants,* by S. P. Tregelles, London, 1851.

sacraments to her, unless she first renounced her faith in the saving grace of Christ. But she remained steadfast in her Evangelical faith.

"What will you do when you have to appear before God, bearing the weight of your sins alone?" the bishop asked her.

The dying prioress replied: *"Having made peace through the blood of His cross, my Saviour has reconciled all things unto Himself in the body of His flesh through death, to present us holy and unblamable and unreprovable in His sight, if we continue in the faith grounded and settled, and not be moved away from the hope of the Gospel."*

She then added, with clasped hands, "In Thee, O Lord, have I trusted, nor wilt Thou suffer the creature that trusts in Thee to be confounded."

The bishop reviled her, but she meekly urged, with tears, that she be permitted to receive the sacraments. He firmly rejected her plea as coming from a "confirmed heretic."

"Well, my Lord," she replied, wiping her eyes, "I am content to bear with resignation whatever deprivation my God sees fit. I am convinced that His divine grace can supply even the want of sacraments."

She fell asleep in the Lord that same night, March 18, 1716, in her seventieth year. Such was the Evangelical spirit of the followers of Jansenius at Port Royal.[2]

---

[2] cf. *The Jansenists, ut supra*, pp. 40-41.

SUFFERINGS AND PERSECUTIONS

The abbess Mère Angelique brought about an Evangelical reformation not only at Port Royal, at the head of which she had been so strangely placed at the age of eleven, but also in many others, such as the rich abbey of Maubuisson, which also had become very corrupt. A group of men famous for their scholarship and piety also became her disciples. Among them may be mentioned Pascal, Le Maitre, Quesnel, Lancelot, Le Maitre de Sacy, Nicole and Singlin.

No fewer than four popes—Urban VII, Innocent X, Alexander VII, and Clement XI—fulminated bulls of excommunication, at the instigation of the Jesuits, against these defenders of Evangelical teachings. They had also against them King Louis XIV of France and his infamous mistress, Madame de Maintenon, Cardinal Richelieu and Cardinal Mazarin. Four French bishops favored and tried to help them. The Dominicans, the Franciscans, and the Benedictines, who to this day still timidly oppose the Jesuits on the teaching of grace, defended the Jansenists of Port Royal as much as they dared. But all the power of the Church of Rome and the King of France was in the hands of the Jesuits, and they used it mercilessly to wipe out every trace of the Jansenists and their Gospel teaching of salvation which they detested and condemned as an "abominable heresy."

Finally, on July 11, 1709, Cardinal de Noailles, archbishop of Paris, was forced by the Pope and the Jesuits to order the complete suppression of the abbey of Port Royal. On the following October 29, the valley was filled with the king's troops, the abbey taken over and the nuns arrested and placed in confinement. The following year the cloister was pulled down; in 1711 the bodies of those buried there were dug up with gross brutality and indecency; two years later the church itself was destroyed. Cardinal de Noailles had ordered it all done according to the bull, *Vineam Domini*, of Pope Clement XI, in which he attacked the doctrines of grace. The cardinal later repented of his deed, and made a visit to the ruins of Port Royal, where on bended knees, he made public testimony of repentance for his weakness. After the death of King Louis XIV and his mistress, Cardinal de Noailles interceded for the imprisoned nuns of Port Royal and had them released.

Jansenism continued in Holland and other countries of Europe after the destruction of Port Royal. Ranke, the historian, says of the Jansenists: *"We find traces of them in Vienna and in Brussels, in Spain and Portugal, and in every part of Italy. They disseminated their doctrines throughout all Roman Catholic Christendom, sometimes openly, often in secret."* [3]

But it was in the Protestant country of Holland that they found best shelter and most freedom. It was there that they were able to organize into a regular Church body under their own bishops. Almost all the Roman Catholics in Holland, to the number of 330,000, at the end of the seventeenth century were Jansenists. The Jesuits had little power there, and they themselves had gone so far in their intrigues and immoral

---

[3] *Op. cit.* p. 45.

teachings that Pope Clement XIV — who had Jansenist sentiments—yielded to the demands of the Catholic countries of Europe and completely abolished the Jesuits in 1773.

CATHOLICS TODAY

Today also there are many sensitive souls within the Roman Catholic Church who sigh for true spirituality and an assurance of salvation that their priests cannot offer. They fear, however, to break with their Church, and continue to accept the sacraments in order to remain in good standing.

Strictly speaking, there is nothing in Roman Catholic teaching to prevent Roman Catholics from professing secretly (*in foro interno*) their faith in the absolute saving power of the Gospel. What is forbidden, under pain of excommunication, is the public profession (*in foro externo*) of such belief.

Thus a Roman Catholic who comes to the true knowledge of Christ, is faced with making the decision of either risking excommunication and the opprobrium of his family and friends by openly professing and demonstrating his faith in Christ as all-sufficient Saviour, or avoiding the penalties by keeping it secret in his heart while conforming outwardly to the rules and ritual as commanded by his Church. But today in America, where freedom of religion is guaranteed to all, no one can be excused if he fails to profess openly his faith in Jesus Christ, who warns (*Matt.* 10: 33): *"Whosoever shall deny me before men, him also will I deny before my Father which is in heaven."*

CHAPTER THIRTY-TWO

SINCE LUTHER

EVERY EFFORT is made by Roman Catholic propagandists in America to discredit the Protestant Reformation and all that has flowed from it during the past four centuries. They insist that it was the greatest tragedy of human history, and trace all the ills of modern life to its influence. Led by the Jesuits and their counter-Reformation, the Catholic Church has never ceased to try to destroy the enlightened order of religious freedom and democracy that has resulted from the revolt of the Christian people in the sixteenth century against the authoritarianism and corruption of the Church of Rome. For if the effects of the Reformation were carried to completion in all countries, not only would religious and civil dictatorship be crushed for ever, but the whole structure of the Roman Catholic Church as now constituted would be threatened with extinction.

The re-discovery and proclamation of the true Christian teaching by Martin Luther and his associates in reality angered the Catholic Church less than their successful attack on the Church's authority and its claim to the absolute control of men and nations. Pope after pope united in a chorus of invective against every extension of religious freedom among the peoples of Europe in the centuries following the Reformation. They feared the end of religious and political authoritarianism and seized every opportunity to bring the nations back again into its grasp.

Their greatest opportunity came with the rise of Fascism after the first World War. Fascism, in fact, is proved to have had its inspiration, if not its actual origin, in the counter-Reformation of the Jesuits. Fascism was Jesuitism with a new label.[1] Coincident with the successes of Franco, Mussolini and Hitler against democracy and freedom that led up to the second World War, Catholic spokesmen in America, echoing Pope Pius XI and his successor Pope Pius XII, began a barrage of abuse against the Protestant Reformation. Their statements left no doubt that they were convinced that Mussolini and Hitler had been sent by God to lead the nations of western civilization back to obedience to the pope. Preaching in St. Patrick's Cathedral in New York on May 5, 1938, Msgr. Michael J. Reilly summarized this effort as follows: *"The Protestant Reformation rejected divine authority, repudiated Christ's sacrificing priesthood, emasculated his sacramental system, his atoning sacrifice of the Mass, and made each a law and a teacher unto himself."*

Cardinal Villeneuve of Canada came especially to Washington shortly after the war broke out and told the National Press Club there on November 16, 1939, that the Protestant Reformation was responsible for the war, that authority and morality had been destroyed by the Protestant revolt "against the authority of the Church of God." He intimated that the

[1] cf. *Behind the Dictators,* and *Vatican Policy in the Second World War,* by L. H. Lehmann, Agora Pub. Co., for factual proofs.

'new order' of Fascism and Nazism was necessary because "four centuries ago certain nations of the North and West of Europe had rejected the authority of the Catholic Church as a divine teacher." Pope Pius XII, in his first encyclical after he became pope, *Summi Pontificatus*, confirmed this by declaring: "*The denial of the fundamentals of morality had its origin in Europe in the abandonment of that Christian teaching, of which the Chair of Peter is the depository and exponent.*" Hitler listened, was greatly encouraged and went ahead with his war of extermination against the Protestant democratic nations.

Cardinal O'Connell of Boston hailed Mussolini as "given to Italy by God." Cardinal Mundelein of Chicago lauded him as follows: "Mussolini is a great big man, the man of the times." Pope Pius XI went further, and in an address to his College of Cardinals on February 13, 1929, styled Mussolini "*the man sent to us by Providence.*"

The near success of this combination of Nazi-Fascism and the Jesuit counter-Reformation in our time had been helped to a certain extent by the failure of the Protestant democratic nations to carry forward the principles of freedom and democracy to their logical conclusion. Protestantism and democracy had become flabby and over-tolerant. They did not push aggressively ahead. They even forgot that eternal vigilance and ever-ready defense were necessary at all times to retain what had been won and passed on to us.

Luther's success was not due to him or to his ideas alone. Back of him was the urge in the Christian people toward universal freedom. Without this, Luther's famous ninety-five theses that he nailed to the door of his church at Wittenberg would have rotted in the rain. Without this God-given urge in the people, hardly an echo of the academic discussions of the theologians that followed would have been heard outside the walls of their universities. If there had not been a quickening of this urge in the people, Luther's challenging theses would have been cast unceremoniously aside, to be forgotten like the charges of other rebellious priests before him. Luther, like them, would have paid for his rashness by doing penance for the rest of his life in the secluded depths of his monastery.

Since it was this urge in the people that had started the Reformation, its complete success could have been secured only by the fullest scope for that urge among the common people. But this seems to have been forgotten. Protestantism and democracy weakened as a consequence in Europe, and at their weakest moment—after the first World War—their age-old enemies, religious and political authoritarianism, struck with devastating effect. The bitter struggle that followed is known to all of us.

Others besides the Roman Catholic propagandists contend that Luther and the other Protestant reformers only hindered the urge for freedom in political and social affairs. Kings, they say, continued to rule in their own right; no real equality was established. After having cast out the demon from the house of God, the reformers, they say, brought him back again with seven other devils more evil than himself who, seeing the house swept and garnished, entered in and took possession of it again.

But this is a grave distortion of the facts. The Protestant Reformation turned out to be not merely an investigation into the maladministration of Christendom and a house-cleaning of the Christian Church. It proved to be something much more important. It resulted in the discovery of something that even the reformers themselves only vaguely suspected was hidden away, as it were, in the celler. Having cleared away the load of papal rubbish which for centuries had been an obstacle to Christian progress, and having drained the sewers of noxious accumulations, they stumbled on the wine of true Christian teaching.

If some of the early Protestant reformers acted strangely, it was not because they had drunk too deeply of this revitalizing wine of Christ. It was rather because they imbibed too little of it. If they erred it was in not allowing this wine to flow freely and gloriously among all peoples. Instead of filling the fountains in the market places with it, they hastened to confine much of it in the musty containers they had inherited from the theologians and law makers of the Church of Rome. They forgot Christ's very important injunction: "No man putteth a piece of new cloth onto an old garment, for that which is put in to fill it up taketh from the garment. Neither do men put new wine into old bottles; else the bottles break, and the wine runneth out, and the bottles perish; but they put new wine into new bottles, and both are preserved."

Luther himself made the mistake of using some of the old terminology of the Roman theologians to explain the working of grace as he saw it. By so doing he limited to a certain extent the full effect of the grace of salvation. Calvin explained the nature of grace with less limitation of its power. He seized upon the musty tomes of Augustine as his prize and carried them out into the light for close scrutiny. He found that there was nothing in Augustine's teachings to uphold the Roman Catholic claim that Almighty God had appointed the pope as his earthly agent of attorney. What he discovered confirmed the Scripture teaching that no man could ever have the power to make the grace of salvation flow into the souls of men, or to retard or withhold it entirely.

It was Calvin's discovery that made Protestantism the bulwark of religious and civil freedom. He established beyond question man's right to approach God directly and personally. His discovery abolished, in the first place, the slave relationship of man to God, and, in the second place, established man's birthright to sonship with God, from which flow those inalienable rights to life, liberty and the pursuit of happiness which make for democracy in the civil order of things.

It has taken the Protestant world four centuries to extend that new relationship of man to God and of man to man to the point where we now find it. That extension is still far from being complete. Those four centuries have been glorious with the dawn that streaked the horizon with hope of religious and political freedom for all men. The struggle has been a bitter and a bloody one. But it cannot be said that the hope has been vain just because the struggle has not been as yet completely successful. The record of the accomplishments of its martyrs, its heroes and nation builders is indelibly inscribed upon the scrolls of history. And that record is a living witness to the truth and effectiveness of the liberating Gospel of Jesus Christ which was reasserted by the Evangelical Christian reformers of the sixteenth century.

It was not so evident to those who started the Reformation, as it is now to us, that what they discovered could not be confined solely to religion. Its effects soon flowed out upon the political and social life of the nations. A reformation was also brought about in the order of relation between government and the governed. It inspired the leaders of the American Revolution and guided the pens of those who signed the Declaration of Independence. It tuned the souls of the French people to the spirit of the Marseillaise. It produced its best effects on the virgin soil of the North American continent where it found its true home.

This was all in keeping with the hoped-for development of the true Christian world order. Christianity is a religion whose true teaching does not support the autocratic control of man over other men in any walk of life. It declares that through Christ all men may have sonship with the same Father, and teaches that virtue is given equally to all. It is entirely opposed to the Roman Catholic doctrine that salvation must be earned as the price of the labor of a hireling, and graded according to the enactments and privileges of Roman law. Above all, it is abhorrent to Christian teaching that the grace of salvation can be granted, without consideration of personal sanctity, as a favor to privileged friends and financial supporters of a mere church organization.

During the first three centuries of Christianity, no hierarchy of church powers, honors and distinctions was admitted. There were 'elders' who acted as spokesmen for the others. A *curia* of cardinals and a *pontifex maximus* were looked upon as institutions of Roman paganism. The early Christians resisted Caesar and his hierarchical gradations of power, and suffered for it. The betrayal came when the elders of the Church in Rome entered into union with the Emperor Constantine for political protection. Later they even assumed Caesar's name of Roman *pontifex*, or high priest. They sinned against the Scripture teaching that in the Christian dispensation Jesus Christ is the one and only high priest, who is *"able to save them to the uttermost who come unto God by him . . . who needeth not daily, as those high priests, to offer up sacrifice, first for his own sins, and then for the people's: for this he did once, when he offered up himself"* (*Heb.* 7: 25, 27).

By so doing these Roman elders robbed the Christian Church of its unique element that makes it altogether different from other religions. For they thus re-established the *imperium* and *sacerdotium*—empire and priesthood—the two elements of the pagan systems of old that Christianity should destroy. Christianity then ceased to function as the Church of the people. From that time on, the Roman pontiffs substituted for the Gospel teaching a legal fiction of the human mediatorship of themselves and their Church between men and God.

This powerful combine of pope and emperor, a system of dual dictators, crushed out the rights of the people redeemed by Christ, both in spiritual and political matters. Caesarism was flavored with the prefix 'holy' and 'Christian'. It was given a new lease of life at the cost of the most precious possession as yet within the grasp of the human race. Soon the popes became powerful enough to rule it over the emperors themselves. They asserted that the power of the spiritual dictator was greater than that of any civil ruler, since the pope held the keys of heaven and hell. Thereafter the emperor became a kind of performing bear dancing to the tune piped by the pope. No emperor could assume power until he was first anointed and crowned by the pope.

What then became of the right of the Christian people to liberty and sonship of God during the centuries from Constantine to Calvin? This right was inalienable and inextinguishable, and did not cease to exist just because the exercise of it was forbidden. The Protestant reformers did not win it for us. It was Christ who won it for us. The Protestant reformers re-discovered it, and the exercise of it has been slowly extended from Calvin's time to our own. Wars and revolutions, with much bloodshed and suffering, have been necessary in order to preserve and further extend it.

What will happen to this Christian right in our new Atomic Era remains to be seen.

CHAPTER THIRTY-THREE

HOOFBEAT AND FOOTFALL

(The end of the beginning)

SENSITIVE SOULS today are burdened with sorrow to behold so much confusion and corruption —those precursors of violence—in every walk of life. And well do we sorrow, for as witnesses for the compassionate Christ we cannot stand apathetically by and watch a maddened world hurtling to destruction.

For, listen—there are ominous hoofbeats in the distance. Do we not hear them quite distinctly now —see the fiery dust rising on the horizon, and feel the earth tremble uneasily! The apocalyptic horsemen are testing their steeds in preparation for their furious ride through the earth. Do our hearts faint within us?

They will, if we do not pause to listen again. But if we have ears that hear we can perceive also a footfall quietly approaching. Above the noise and confusion of this impenitent world and the dreadful hoofbeats of the impatient steeds, we can hear the footfall of the Beloved, the soft footfall of our blessed Lord. He promised never to leave us or forsake us.

> *Do we not hear Thy footfall, O Beloved,*
> *Among the stars on many a moonless night*
> *Do we not catch the whisper of Thy coming . . .*

There is something glorious in the thought that were the Christian Church, from Pentecost down, to form one vast circle around our Lord, our hands might possibly clasp those of the very beginning. *They* faced martyrdom and sealed their testimony with their blood. *Our* task now is as hard as theirs. We need "patience and contentedness with Christ's approbation, keeping His word, not denying His name" in the midst of the monstrous indifference to His claims, the insolent idolatry and all the swirling forces of evil.

There is something tremendously inspiring in the fact that for centuries now the reapers have been gathering in the sheaves, and that it is our privilege to be out in the field to bring in the final gleanings while the darkness lowers fast.

There is a sense of hurry in the air, as there always is before a gathering storm. We must not take time to be shut up to sorrow—rather the sorrow must be closed up in us while quickly we work (*Ps.* 126: 6).

What encouragement is there for the present hour? Even in the valley of Baca (weeping) is found refreshment, and we can pass through it going "from strength to strength." Tarry at Dothan and behold the mountain full of horses and chariots of fire and be told again that "they that be with us are more than they that be with them." Then climb to the "secret of the stairs" and hear the God of all comfort say, *"I will see you again, and your heart shall rejoice, and your joy no man taketh from you"* (*John* 16: 22).

For the joy of the Lord is our strength, and in His strength and joy let us watch and work and wait.

Neither should the brief apparent triumph of culminating evil tempt us to retreat for an instant from the conflict and sink the soul in defeat; nor should any ecstasy of thought of soon-coming glory exempt us from the burden of this perishing world and care for the souls of men.

But as the hoof-beats draw nearer, know this assuredly, so also does the footfall.

And we, caught up in the air
Shall see Thee, O Beloved, we shall see Thee,
In hush of adoration see Thee there.

Poem by Amy Carmichael.